The Calling

By: Jacob Terán

The Calling

The Calling is a riveting story of a young Chicano's journey in discovering his own identity with decisions he must make on his own. A coming-of-age story of a young Chicano man whose barrio filled with gangs, drugs, and violence pushed him to explore his own identity. Completely focused on joining the Marine Corps after dropping out of high school and occupying a juvenile detention center, Guillermo Tierra grapples with societal obstacles to reach a goal. When external issues arise that Tierra cannot join the Marine Corps at first, he must make a decision that will ultimately alter the trajectory of his life. Moreover, the audience follows the protagonist, Guillermo Tierra, into multiple worlds that reveal the layers to his character, upbringing, and ambitions to becoming who he ultimately sees himself when life does not go as planned. When college becomes a potential pathway to joining the military, critical thinking and his Chicano identity allow him to reconsider what his calling in life may be.

The Calling
© 2025 Jacob Terán
ISBN: 9781966337089
First Edition, 2025
Library of Congress Control Number: 2025917265

Printed in the United States of America

Edited by: Jacob Terán
Cover Design by: Dulce López-Terán
Layout Design by: Erica Castro

Dedication

This book is dedicated to Alicia and Dulce. Two of the strongest women that I know. Without you both, I would not be where I am at.

These lines of poetry are dedicated to every single person, family, friend, or stranger I have shared positive energy in some form, shape, or manner. They are also dedicated to everyone who believed in me and those that didn't. It made a difference.

its ups and down. Teran takes it on in his own unvarnished voice, the life he's known in greater L.A. with its ups and downs, Chicano style, inflected with cholo slang and college smarts. It's an honest read, with plenty of trouble for Guillermo, and hope at the end.

-Stephen D. Gutierrez, author of *Captain Chicano Draws a Line in the American Sand*

The Calling by Jacob Teran is a narrative that presents Guillermo, a young Chicano who lives with traumas from both the past and present, seeking answers to what he sees, hears, and experiences. The voices that come from the people closest to him, his community, the societal institutions, and his past all surround him. Guillermo listens and is influenced by the voices calling to him, but he learns to listen to his own voice. *The Calling* gives an excellent story of the millions of young Chicanos and Chicanas who find themselves in the same situation today, eager to find their own calling. This story is significant for our time!

-Alejandro Morales, author of *Barrio on Edge*, *River Angels*, *Little Nations & Other Stories*

Land Acknowledgment

I acknowledge that the land we occupy is located within the traditional homelands occupied by the Gabrielenos/ Tongva (People of the Earth), the Toongvetam. We also acknowledge the Gabrielenos/ Tongva as the traditional and Indigenous people to live on this land. We respect and value the many ways the Gabrieleno/ Tongva cultural heritage and beliefs continue to have significance today. We also acknowledge and are reminded of the sacred and spiritual relationship that has always existed here in Los Angeles County not only for the Gabrieleno/ Tongva, but for their neighbors, the Chumash (Seashell People), the Payomkawichum (People of the West), Tataviam (People of the Mountains), the Yuhaaviatam clan of Maara'yam (People of the Pines), the Cahuilla (Powerful Ones), and all other Indigenous people across stolen land and sea.

Acknowledgments

I wish to acknowledge a few people who made this novella possible. First, my wife, Dulce López-Teran. I love you very much, baby. Without you, I would not have the courage to start and continue my writing, let alone publish any of my work. I also want to acknowledge Stephen Gutierrez, Alejandro Morales, Scott Russell Duncan, and Edna Campos Gravenhorst. The inspiration you have given me in each of your unique ways has provided me the push and fuel to write for mi comunidad y mi gente. Gracias por todo. Tlazokamati. Lastly, I would like to thank Erica Castro (Lopez) for working with me to publish my book. I am also thankful for the opportunity to be invited and speak with your students. You have all made this possible and I could not be more grateful for the connection I have with you all.

Preface

This novella started out as a 4-page assignment for a creative writing class. I just graduated with my associates degree from Rio Hondo Community College and was focused on becoming a college professor. The funny thing is how I ended up in college and this story paints a picture as to how an unlikely journey was made possible.

Ever since I started college, I wanted more literature on people that looked like me; that lived my experience or something similar. I grew curious and wondered if it was possible that there were any writers that grew up in the barrio or even close to that vicinity, or close to me. That is where I came across Steve Gutierrez's to where I reached out to him. Not only was he friendly and helpful, but Gutierrez also sent me his *Elements* and *The Mexican Man in His Backyard* and personally signed it. This gave me so much inspiration to continue writing that I published my first short story "A Quiet Night on the Boulevard" on Somos en Escrito where it can still be found as of 2025. I reached out to Alejandro Morales who authored many books, who was also from the East Los Angeles area. Morales shared the same generosity and nurturing as Gutierrez to a young writer such as myself and I believe these two Chicano writers from the Los Angeles area made a huge impact on me. Knowing they both lived in nearby barrios, were Chicanos, and published books that I've come to love and admire had a direct impact on working on more literature for our Gente. Now more than ever, we need more literature for students, people, and families to relate, empathize, and be inspired. I write for many reasons, but this one is a major one. I want our Gente to know there are more like us that have stories to share.

"...I am Cuauhtémoc, proud and noble,
leader of men, king of an empire civilized
beyond the dreams of the gachupín Cortés,
who also is the blood, the image of myself.
I am the Maya prince.
I am Nezahualcóyotl, great leader of the Chichimecas.
I am the sword and flame of Cortes the despot
And I am the eagle and serpent of the Aztec civilization.
I owned the land as far as the eye
could see under the Crown of Spain,
and I toiled on my Earth and gave my Indian sweat and
blood
for the Spanish master who ruled with tyranny over man
and
beast and all that he could trample
But...THE GROUND WAS MINE..."

-Rodolfo Corky Gonzales, "I am Joaquin"

The Calling

Table of Contents

Part I

Part II

Part III

Part IV

Part I

CHAPTER ONE

G et the fuck up, right now!! A cheap, beat-up and bent aluminum trash can lid is suddenly battered repeatedly with a recruit's stolen shoe. Lights as blinding as the sun's solar rays abruptly awake those from their slumber. The handmade alarm clock ushers shock and awe as utter chaos ensues at 4 in the morning. Multiple men known as Marines acting as drill instructors run with hands behind their waists and noses viciously attacking their line of vision – competing with postures of tyrannosaurus rexes – down the aisles of bunks that house young men known as recruits.

Teenagers between the tender age of 13 and 17's "I-know-everything-about-the world" awake frantically trying to make their beds and find their shoes. One Marine, 3rd platoon leader Sergeant Graves, flips the bottom bunk mattress of an unsuspecting recruit that was still putting on his shoes not to the Sergeant's speedy satisfaction. A few recruits were crying since many have never been yelled at before by someone with eyes bulging out of their sockets and saliva spraying their faces. The majority continued to scramble due to the stampeding verbal barrage of tyrant lizards making them second guess what they should do next. A lesser number of recruits were standing in a position of attention in front of the bunk's storage because they paid attention. Guillermo Tierra is among those few, a street-smart kid from the barrio who has experienced some things other teens his age shouldn't have. Being within a stressful environment is something Tierra is not unfamiliar to. He is locked in like a bronze statue, focused, partly because of fear, but mostly because of the chaotic excitement.

The bald, dark complected marine with eyes as sharp as his knife hands gestures to a recruit. "Lock it up, Tierra!" Sergeant Grave's knife's hands being centimeters away from Tierra's right cheek allowed the recruit to smell the aloe vera hand sanitizer on the Sergeant's fingertips.

"Aye, sir!" Tierra shouts.

"Whaaat? I can't hear you, recruit! Sound the fuck off!!" The Sergeant replaces his razor fingers with his own laser eyes right next to Tierra's face to make him flinch.

"AYE, SIR!!!" Tierra is careful not to flinch and thinks it is amazing to be yelled at, only to yell back even louder and not be reprimanded.

"That's better recruit! Don't fuck it up as I saw how fucking slow you got out of my bunk onto my floor! Stop moving so fucking slooow!!"

"Yes, sir, Sergeant Graves, sir!!" Tierra shouts loud enough for the late-20-something-year-old Sergeant to move on.

Just as Sergeant Graves was about to harass the recruit adjacent to Tierra, a 15-year-old boy across the way exclaims how sorry he was to another Marine drilling him. Graves flew next to his colleague to berate the child.

"Recruit, are you friends with Corporal Ericson? HUH?! ANSWER NOW, RECRUIT!!" Sergent Graves stands like a prehistoric bipedal monster hovering over his prey ready to pounce.

"…N-n-no, s-sir," the wide-eyed young recruit's knees were shaking.

"Then why the fuck are you saying sorry FOR?!!"
The Sergeant leans in as if the smell of fear and uncertainty
satiated him.

"...I don't k-know, s-sir. I'm sorry!" The recruit's
eyebrows rise high as if they were at gunpoint.

"Are we drinking buddies?! STOP FUCKING SAY-
ING SORRY BEFORE I GIVE YOU A REASON!!!"

"Y-yes, s-sir!!" The young kid managed to shout.

Several Marines heard the kid and soar like a wake
of vultures smelling the blood of vulnerability. In this
realm, *their domain as they would say*, vulnerability is
not necessarily seen as a weakness of sorts, but an area to
improve on as this cult sees any signs of vulnerability as a
weak spot to the unit as a whole; at least that is what Tierra
was taught to believe since the first day he came here. The
Marines, including Sergeant Graves, all gather around the
uncertain teenager while banging aluminum trash can lids
centimeters away from his ears, all the while making the
kid sound off louder. This went on until the kid turned red,
barely able to breathe from exhaustion. All the other recruits stand upright facing each other across their bunks as
they melt each other with their own laser eyes, not daring to
look at any Marine who could send them to the fifth circle
of hell, if this wasn't the lobby to such a place.

Tierra is scared but also mixed with excitement
because today was the last day of this place. Still, he could
not believe he was doing something he has been wanting
to do for some time now. In a matter of a year, he would
be able to enlist into the real thing, the Marine Corps. To
serve his country? To redeem himself from the trouble he
got himself into and anguish his mother endured? Maybe to
better his life because nothing else could pull him out of the
hell of his own barrio of eventually joining a gang or get
locked up? He wasn't certain of any of these thoughts, but
all Tierra did know was *this* path would change his life

–hopefully for the better. This Junior Marine encampment is the test to that path and Tierra is keeping afloat, actually, treading the water fine. Yet at the same time, he wishes he could still enjoy the juvenile freedom of a delinquent with no responsibilities as he once did. Sometimes, he wishes he could go back to selling half pounds of sticky, skunky marijuana. Or stealing his mom's car to go on joy rides around Boyle Heights and East Los Angeles. But Tierra knows if he continues on that path, it will lead him to the horrific and unpleasant examples he's already seen in his barrio. Tierra flashes back into the recent past as the controlled chaos pauses for a few seconds.

CHAPTER TWO

The night two weeks before the military encampment was like any other night. Guillermo just got out of juvenile hall almost two months ago and went back to doing the same activities that lead him in there: truancy from high school, experimenting with different drugs he thought would help him reach some type of higher consciousness with the cholos and cholo wannabes in his barrio, theft ranging from petty to stealing cars – all sorts of mamadas that did not interfere with his own moral compass. But something happened during his juvenile detention center occupancy; A realization as to how "good" he was at being a criminal – he thought he could perhaps pivot that ill production of life to something positive or worthwhile. He felt and knew his life was being wasted on potential that could be put to some use or purpose, but nothing came to mind he could do other than "posting up" in his neighborhood. The difficulty of living a debaucherous lifestyle, the role models in Guillermo's barrio who had issues of their own, along with living in a single-family apartment in a lower socioeconomic environment, all contributed to his surroundings and choices.

Guill learned that he wanted to join the Marine

Corps while he was incarcerated. He thought that the Corps would redeem his honor from all the horrendous things he was doing in his barrio – hanging with current and future cholos, disobeying his mother, selling marijuana, and doing things that would have easily sent him in youth authority until he was 18 if he'd been caught. He also knew that one day, all the fun and danger he indulged in would come to an end, or not, only time could tell, and he could not see that far into his future, nor did he care.

While incarcerated, he began calisthenics in his shared unit with 3 other boys that made it a routine and read more – two things Guill did not care to do all the while staying in las calles. Aside from working out for the first time for himself, he found reading to be just as difficult, almost the same way it was to get into a routine with physically strengthening his body. Like all muscles, Guillermo had to condition his mind to focus on the words he was reading. As a child, a very fond memory of his mom reading to him after she came home from work, lives on in his mind. Guillermo specifically remembers the vivid images of a cat and dog doing meaningless actions while his mother helped him pronounce the verbs and adjectives, he was new to learning. But more than learning parts of speech, he remembers the images that played within his mind – his imagination. Almost as if a movie was occurring through a lens, he could vaguely see the dog jumping or the cat sleeping. This led him to checking out several books, but none caught his attention, except for one – Robert Mason's narrative of his time as a helicopter pilot in Vietnam.

Chickenhawk was fascinating, in regard to plot, setting, and characters, but perhaps the main reason he stayed with the book was because it reminded him of his father. Guillermo's dad was there for him throughout his life, but he was also wrestling with his own demons from his past. The Marine Veteran who served in the highest casualty era of Vietnam in 1969, experienced a lot of traumas before and after being drafted. Born as a 2nd generation Mexican American, Guillermo's father, Mauricio, was taught to suppress his first language in school by teachers, white kids, and coconuts alike, and ultimately, his identity. In the 1950s-60s, being a wetback and beaner were the last things any dark skinned Mexican wanted to be known as. This assimilation affected many men and women, boys and girls like Guill's father and abuelo. Guillermo's abuelo also served in the U.S. Army in the Pacific Theatre of World War II, making the assimilation to American culture that much easier along with the ongoing racism that took place throughout the Valley – north of Los Angeles. Choices were made when the draft came as some of Mauricio's friends tried to persuade their friend to dodge the draft by heading to Mexico or Canada. Many exclaimed the Vietnam War was no place for a Chicano, but Mauricio did not feel like a Chicano. He was an *American* and *needed to serve his country*, just like his father did. He needed to *prove his worth as a proud American*. The assimilation he had not much control of, but his choice to fulfil his civil draft duties lead Mauricio to Vietnam.

In four years' time, seeing combat as a door gunner on a CH-46 Chinook, witnessing bodies from both sides get shredded like paper, Mauricio left the war with PTSD. However, performing his duties without question led Mauricio to also earning rank as Sergeant. Like his father before him, Mauricio put all his energy into his work, and the apple did not fall far from the tree for Guillermo. The combination of Mauricio's PTSD, work ethic that led to a fruitful career as a foreman with construction, contributed to the mild emotional and physical neglect for Guill. But regardless, he loved his son very much and Guill the same for his father.

This journey of the Tierra family could perhaps

partially explain why Guillermo would even fathom joining the Marines. After all, Guill never liked the police, and the military was never something that impressed him growing up. But the lineage of the men in his family and service to their country was always something taught to Guill when he was little – a form of assimilation that always stayed in the back of his mind. But of all the changes that were taking place within Guillermo's mind during his incarceration, nothing affected him more than a conversation he had with a bunkie – a roommate he shared vulnerable and secret feelings with. A nightly conversation with a 17-year-old kid named Roy Zaragosa stood with Guillermo for the reminder of the months he was in juvenile hall.

Like the military, within jails, prisons, and juvenile halls for the labeled delinquents and disturbed, most addressed people by their last name.

"So, I been meaning to ask you Zaragosa, what are you going to do once you get out of this shit hole? Jones, Lopez, and Ramirez and I were all saying how dope that shit would be to go to Venice Beach, roll up some fat ass joints, and burn all our shit from this place in a bonfire. Get faded, maybe even kick it with some hynas," Tierra laughs as he could imagine everything to how the beach would smell and sound all on a warm LA summer evening.

Zaragosa heard the conversation many times with different guys. "Nah, man, I'm enlisting in the Marines."

"The *Marines*, like the Marine Corps, *Marines*?" Tierra was confused to hear something so odd.

Zaragosa smiles back knowing it's not the typical answer most kids locked up say what they want to do when they leave these confined walls of deprivation and failed system of rehabilitation. "Yeah, right when I get out, I'll be meeting a recruiter, take the ASVAB, and ship off to boot camp if everything goes as planned. Which it should from what the recruiter told me," Zaragosa's confidence pulled

Tierra in.

"But what about your folks, don't you want to see them? Get faded one last time? Other family or homies?" Tierra could not help but wonder, especially knowing that Zaragosa had foster parents. Still, even knowing Zaragosa had people that were not his biological parents, Tierra could not fathom seeing family one last time or experiencing one more night of some hedonistic debaucherous fun.

"I thought a lot since I first got here. I want to do something with my life. Working out, traveling the world for free, and getting paid for it – it's a lot better than the bullshit I was doing at home," Zaragosa spoke honestly with Tierra because he trusted him. Tierra also knew what led Zaragosa inside their jail.

Zaragosa got into a bad fight with a neighbor in his city of Long Beach. The cops came and restrained both the neighbor and Zaragosa. Zaragosa's foster parents pleaded with him to stop being rebellious, but the neighbor called him a spick and spit on his leg, falsely accusing him of stealing their 11-year-old daughter's bike. The police made Zaragosa sit down on the graffiti-filled curb and interlock his legs. The two police officers spoke with the neighbors to get a report and see if they wanted to file charges for aggravated assault and battery. In a split second and for what reason nobody will ever know, Zaragosa snapped, darted like a comet into the unlocked police cruiser. The police saw the comet's tail and tried to pursue his trail but to no avail. Zaragosa managed to put the cruiser into drive and accelerate, but only to be yanked out while the cruiser continued down the street, resulting in the vehicle crashing into another parked vehicle and finally a tree. A very different sort of crime from Tierra, but all the young men here in this juvenile rehabilitation center have their own war stories of what they've done. Many were proud and still claimed the gang they got jumped into, rebelling all authority any chance they got. Others, like Zaragosa, were reflecting on why they were there. Some wished to continue doing the things that brought them here, while a small number wanted some kind of transformation – Zaragosa was one of the rare types and it inspired Tierra to consider the latter group.

Tierra and Zaragosa talked about how life would be by changing their troubled lives, filled with trauma from their own young lives and their parents before them. Asking *what-ifs*, wondering if redemption could be possible not in the eyes of a religious god, but in the eyes of their parents; of themselves. Deep down, both Tierra and Zaragosa knew they fucked up beyond any typical adolescent's mistake such as talking back to a parent or staying out too late. But a splinter stayed lodged in both their minds, scratching their prefrontal cortex if they can ever regain confidence to be like "normal" people. This conversation had a profound effect on Tierra as he did not have another male friend to share vulnerability in his barrio before. The closest thing Tierra shared experiences with homeboys in his hood was getting high and talking about shallow topics of reputation and short-lived pleasures. Any ounce of vulnerability or shared emotions meant you were soft, lacking of one's own masculinity, which nobody would ever dare sacrifice. Strength and machismo reigned superior and even when Tierra did not feel strong, he like his other homeboys faked it – too many youngsters learn this in the hood.

Soon enough, it was Tierra's time to come back home from his incarceration and back into society. Guillermo was tempted and knew he might go back to doing the same stuff that led him inside his incarceration. He still indulged in a few recreational drugs here and there, still committed petty theft, and sold weed, but could not engage in other more serious crimes like he used to, let alone look for the opportunities. It could be argued that the young Guillermo did gain some introspection while off the streets. While confined, one of his favorite novels aside from Mason's *Chickenhawk* was *A Clockwork Orange* and like the protagonist of the story, Guillermo knew he shared the same sentiment of being "cured all right" – it would be a matter of time before indulging in the next moment of opportunity.

About a month out of his juvenile detention, Guillermo thought about trying out the Junior Marines – a 14-day encampment where actual Marines from the Marine Corps take on the role as drill instructors and attempt to instill discipline in young people within Camp Pendleton, San Diego. Guill's conversation with Zaragosa rang true in his mind and Guill also wanted to change his life. Guillermo did not know what to expect but all he knew was that he would miss getting high in his barrio and indulging in the debauchery of his streets he was all too familiar with.

CHAPTER THREE

Tierra time travels to the last night he had before being woken up *here* by eye-bulging and razor-handed Marines. The chaos of the bipedal screaming lizards provides coverage to zone in and out of his current reality. The night before waking up to this experience –a night of smoking marijuana blunts and chasing it down with cold Red Stripe brews with one of his few homies – Mad Mike. The maddest half Mexican, half white boy Tierra knew.

"This shit smell DANK!!" Mike gave a villainous laugh staring into oblivion that was the dirty windshield of his grandmother's van he would take to smoke with Guillermo.

"Tell me about it. The homie hooked it up… You ready to fly to the dark side of the moon?" Guillermo knew he could say the goofiest shit he wanted and did not have to worry about being made fun of for being himself around Mike. Guill passed the lighter for Mike to spark the plump rolled tobacco wrap that snuggly hugged the sticky marijuana.

Mad Mike was given the name on account that he was "crazy" in the most literal sense. Schizophrenia had affected his mother's side and it got passed down to Mike.

His smile was something contagious that would either make you feel joyful or worried, but never in between. Sometimes Guillermo would picture Mike co-starring alongside a 90's Jim Carrey movie as Mike's enthusiastic smile would match the infamous, "Alrighty then" actor. Guillermo felt comfortable around him and perhaps it was because they both enjoyed smoking marijuana together and listening to 60's psychedelic music. Guillermo pondered on whether it was their common denominator of getting high and taste of music, or if it was because they both felt like they were not accepted into society for their social deviancy. Most likely both.

But Guillermo is no longer there in the *outside* world getting high with his schizophrenic homeboy who was constantly not taking his meds, (who shouldn't have been smoking weed either), and he is *no longer* Guillermo. He is *here* among the mighty few and proud dinosaurs attacking recruits with bad hygienic saliva, and *he is* Tierra in their prehistoric world of rank and power. Tierra wishes he could have just one more day sleeping in his filthy bed he never cleaned for weeks that his mother constantly and rightfully scolded. Or going on a joy ride in his mom's car while her ignorance fueled the delinquent joy in it. Or simply just one more day to hang out with his proclaimed homies, including Mad Mike. But Tierra is here now, and it is his last day in this militaristic encampment for young men. The comfort of a friend's mad smile is now replaced with a mad devil dinosaur (or devil dog as they like to be called) and it's violently screaming while saliva flies in various areas of Tierra's face.

"Atten-HUH!!! …Lock that shit up!!" The Sergeant and his colleagues stood with precisive readiness as Graves did the morning announcements. "Okay you sad bunch of disappointing shits! Today is your last day in my beloved barracks," everything that is in the Marine Corps base, including the land was *theirs*. "Get your camping shit because anything you leave here you ain't getting back."

The recruits, including Tierra have 5 minutes to pack all of their belongings that they used for the past 2 weeks into their backpacks and not a second to spare. The recruits and Marines were going up "Ol' Smokey" – a vast and steep mountain within Camp Pendleton that actual recruits from the Marine Corps hike up at the end of their boot camp, hauling around 50 pounds. It is a test of mind, body, and soul to weed out the people that *cannot* do it, since all Marines could do anything, according to myths. Because Tierra and his fellow recruits were a part of this program for adolescents, they only carried 25 pounds, which consists of their backpack, a sleeping bag, clothes, water canteen and some sealed food known as MREs.

After eating breakfast in the prison-like chow hall, all the recruits rushed back to their barracks to pick up their backpack for they were to not only trek up Ol' Smokey, but they were also all going to camp tentless under the blanket of the stars. All the recruits' nerves were shot as many did not sleep well and stress was brought to an all-time high. From being yelled out every day to pushing their bodily limits, this was the final test – the recruits have to climb up *their* mountain. The ascent was brutal as the sun felt like it was as close as the moon, in addition to Tierra not used to hiking, let alone carrying a 25-pound backpack. There were 6 platoons – groups of 40 or so recruits led by a platoon leader who is a Sergeant from the Marines. Throughout the climb, many recruits need to stop and rest, halting all other platoons, which Tierra is grateful for. Stop, go, stop, go, stop, go. As the hike went on, it began to hurt more to stop and continue shortly after. With sore shoulders from the straps of the pack, sore feet accompanied by blisters from unbroken boots, and overall exhaustion, Tierra and his platoon finally reached the plateau just before the summit.

The Sergeants of each platoon readied their recruits to their areas where they would sleep, creating boundaries made of rocks, dirt, and plastic barrels that other Marines brought driving up the fire road in military flatbed trucks. MREs, or Meals Ready to Eat, are dispersed to each recruit for supper as the sun begins to rest along the Pacific Ocean horizon. It is a beautiful sight to behold, and Tierra basks in the view as he has never seen the sun and ocean touch before, almost as if these two celestial giants kiss.

Baker, a recruit in the same 4th platoon as Tierra looks with disgust at his own beige bagged MRE. "I cannot wait to have some real food when I get outta' here," Baker looks towards Tierra knowing he hears him.

Tierra quickly and discreetly eyeballs which MRE Baker was so grossed out on. "Well, we ain't out yet, so until then, if you don't want your chili & mac, I'll gladly take that off you," Tierra offers.

"I'll trade you. What do you have to offer?" Baker speedily requests.

Tierra hides the food with his current MRE of hashbrown potatoes with bacon bag to his side, as it's one of the favorite MREs among everyone. Tierra keeps an old MRE visible he got the first week from another recruit that was stubborn as a mule about his food like Baker. Tierra always switches the MREs of something he doesn't like with a bag that others wanted, since MREs were randomly dispersed. Tierra has some lemon pepper tuna which was not a favored MRE among Marines as well as the recruits here and slips it in his hashbrown potatoes with bacon bag.

"I got this shitty potatoes and bacon MRE. I really don't care for it," Tierra offers the bag out towards Baker.

"Shit, for real?! Haha! Here take mine!" Baker laughs at what appears as sheer stupidity as he tries to snag the trade out of Tierra's hand, but Tierra is faster.

"Ah, ah. Hand me yours, first," Tierra learned a lot

about transactions growing up in his barrio and you never let someone snatch something from your hands.

"Fine, here! Shit, you think I was going to just steal it from you," Baker laughs.

Baker reminded Tierra of that loud kid in the playground who acted tough but would run away with his tail between his legs as soon as someone stands up. Sure, he was a bit bigger and taller than Tierra, but being inside a juvenile rehabilitation center and growing up the way he did, it can have a keen effect on most adolescents to measure who and what is in fact, a threat. The overconfident recruit took off to sit with some other recruits to show them the great trade he got from Tierra. Tierra knew that if you traded, it was at your own risk, so any potential complaint from Baker would fall on himself for agreeing. Tierra enjoys his food as he watched the last inches of the sun's beams that zigzagged across the ocean knowing he was going to rest well tonight with a full and satisfied stomach.

Tierra marveled at the beauty of the night. He learned some time ago that the very stars he is looking at this very moment are the same stars his ancestors from 500 years ago were most likely looking at. Tierra always appreciated the mysteries of the universe as it felt much grander than religion, especially the Judao-Christian version of god – unrestricted by dogma and boundaries, limitless and infinite possibilities that no being could ever fathom. Just as Tierra fixates on a star that he imagines an ancestor of his was looking at 5 centuries ago, he is interrupted by a volley of a crimson metal rainstorm. Piercing red laser beams shoot out from a far distance somewhere off in a desolate area of Camp Pendleton. Hundreds of these lava-like projectiles shoot from a flying machine creating this shocking display of death from above. Tierra is in shock and awe as he could not look away. Even the sound of what spews out from this metal beast was overwhelming.

Tierra along with Baker and his peers all quietly watch. Young men who are believed to be destined to maybe one day fly that machine and bring some form of dignified justice for this country, all gaze silently. But what crosses the minds of every young man at this very second as they watch this violent display of romanticized bravado is, *why*? What happens to someone who gets in that line of fire? Are families with the enemy when that crimson metal rainstorm hails down from above? Are there any enemies of the U.S. that are worthy of such a display of tyrannical power? But most of all, why? There are no hoorays or hoorahs, just utter silence, as this beastly dragon of all dragons' surges hellfire across the distance.

Tierra is not necessarily proud of the war machine that he sees either. Is joining the military a way out of the hood? Absolutely. But at what cost on oneself and at what cost of others? The image of something unnatural created by man in contrast to the environment being part of the natural world pushes Tierra to further ponder on whether enlisting is the right choice. *America are the good guys, right? They wouldn't have all this stuff if they weren't, right?...* Such power under the disposal of man or one nation is overwhelming for Tierra to consider. The red lasers may look beautiful to some – a sheer absolute display of power, but so is the wonder of gazing at the same balls of light his ancestors did before him. So, he turns to look at the celestial heavens and becomes lost to how small this country and its firepower really is compared to the cosmos above.

The next morning, MRE chow is dispersed as all the recruits gathered and cleaned up their areas before leaving. Tierra gestures his MRE bag to Baker to see if he was open to trading to where Baker replies with a smirk, his middle finger, and slowly mouthing, "fuck you." Tierra could not help but laugh, opens his bag, and chows down. Today was the summit of Ol' Smokey. No one knows what to expect except to see some kind of view of sorts, especially since they all knew the ocean was not far. The last of the ascent was not as bad for Tierra as it was only about 500 ft of elevation gain in under half an hour, unlike the death march from the day before of 1,800 ft. in under ¾ of a mile. None of the Marines accompanying the recruits were out of breath, however, every single recruit was gasping for air since everyone was pushed to go fast on account the summit was not far from their sleeping grounds. But there they all are, finally, at the top.

The Marine Drill Sergeants from each platoon sound off attendance for all recruits to stand in position of attention, rows of ten, and columns of 4. The Marines then move boxes from their trucks to the ground of something each recruit tries to see by their newly learned skill of using their peripheral. No recruits can see what the Marines are taking off the trucks as they have been drilled to not move from their position of attention like their lives depended on it.

It was then learned that this summit was the recruit's acknowledgment by their Drill Sergeants before officially graduating – a type of "You-are-still-a-little-piece-of-shit-but-good-for-you-for-making-it-to-the-end-you-little-piece-of-shit," congratulations. Each Drill Sergeant from each platoon visits each recruit in serious fashion without smiles or praise. Most interactions were fast, some took a few more seconds, and some were a bit longer. Tierra was up next.

"At-ease, recruit," a mellow yet serious tone comes from Sergeant Graves.

"Aye, Sergeant," Tierra wants to shout but did not sense the need to.

Sergeant Graves dug into his pocket and gestured Tierra to his hand, a coin, commemorating the completion of his encampment. "Do you know why I did not make you a squad leader, Tierra?"

"No, sir."

"The reason I chose to not make you a squad leader was because of the discipline you possessed from day one. You moved with speed and intensity and always took the initiative, even when you knew nobody was looking. You already had discipline in you and most of all… Most of all, Tierra, because you are already a fucking goddamn leader. Don't let that fucking shit go to your head either. You still got a lot to improve on and you better continue excelling in whatever the fuck you do. Don't waste your life. Congratulations."

There were no hugs, no smiles, it was all transactional. As quickly as Sergeant Graves came in front of Tierra, he was gone to the next recruit. As Tierra processes what his Platoon Leader told him, Tierra stared straight into the ocean. "*Don't waste your life.*" Almost as if Sergeant Graves was telling him to find a way out of his neighborhood. It could also be as if the Sergeant was telling Tierra to not waste his life by joining the Marines. There is no way Tierra will ever know what Sergeant Graves meant, but it didn't matter. A marginal tear manifests from Tierra's left eye and a proud, choked mutter came out, "…thank you, Sergeant."

Part II

CHAPTER FOUR

Three months after graduating from the Junior Marines, Tierra finally built up the courage to speak to a recruiter in his hometown of East Los Angeles. The cross streets of Beverly Boulevard and Wilcox Avenue was home to the Monte Plaza – the local DMV, several mom and pop shops that sold Mexican food, pizza, and pastries, and in the corner, a suite of recruiters from the Army, Navy, and Marine Corps could all be found here. Down the street from the plaza was Wilcox Elementary where Tierra went to school. This area of East Los Angeles felt like home to Tierra more than anything, giving him that much more confidence to enter through the recruiter's office.

The recruiters inside were cordial and inviting, after all, their job is to recruit young men and women, and such a job should be carried out with grace and charm. On this day, Staff Sergeant Cocho resides inside by himself. A Marine whose been in the Corps for 10 years or so as a military vehicle mechanic, which was a job closely dangerous to infantry and artillery. He looks white-passing but with his name, he might have been Puerto Rican or some other ethnicity of Raza. Tierra couldn't tell his genetic makeup or where he grew up, but he never saw his sort of name before.

"Hello sir, welcome! How can I help today?" The mid-30s recruiter is as friendly as can be.

"Umm, yeah…I'm not sure how the process works," Tierra looks around the red-painted room, spotting a pull-up bar, most likely the recruiter's gym bag, some dirty socks, regalia laying idly, and motivational posters that screamed in large black and gold font, "THE FEW, THE PROUD, THE MARINES."

"Cool, where you from? Are you also thinking about enlisting as I can surely help you with any questions," all smiles came from Staff Sergeant Cocho.

"I'm from East LA. It's pronounced 'Co-cho,' que no?" Tierra could see the name on his desk.

"Spot on bro! For people that can't pronounce it, I say like the number in Spanish, 'ocho.' But some still can't say it," the Staff Sergeant lets out a gentle chuckle.

Both the recruiter and Tierra sit down at an aluminum desk and iron out the steps and process of what needs to be done to enlist. The Staff Sergeant is cordial and approachable to what Tierra feels and thinks to be quite awesome for a person who is both a Marine and a recruiter. Tierra still kept his guard up as he heard from different people that recruiters are sharks and are only trying to persuade you to enlist for their own benefit – no different from a car salesman. This appeared to be evident once both came to the conversation of Tierra's high school completion, education being a minimal requirement, and it is an issue.

Every recruiter not only has a quota to "recruit" a certain number of bodies to become a part of America's fighting elite, but they also receive more merit if the potential recruit graduated from high school, has no criminal record, and has outstanding ASVAB (Armed Services Vocational Aptitude Battery) test scores, all of which Tierra has none of. Tierra in an instant becomes the most unattractive recruit for not only did he spend half a year in juvenile rehabilitation center but was also a high school dropout.

"This is standard bro, lets have you go into our room to take a practice ASVAB test. Just read the instructions and do your best. I'll be in the room right over if you need anything," Cocho eases Tierra into the recruiter's testing room near the entrance door.

Taking the practice ASVAB test shows the Staff Sergeant that Tierra was not the most effective at taking academic exams. Sure, Tierra mentions he was a part of the Junior Marines, but Cocho could care less about Tierra's accomplishments as his job of recruiting ideal candidates was much more important for his own reputation. Cocho is more concerned about whether Tierra could help with his yearly recruiter quota. The more Tierra spoke to Cocho about his life and goals in confidence, Cocho judged too many discrepancies compared to Tierra's 18-year-old counterparts who some were stellar sports athletes or eggheads who were taking colleges classes in high school.

"Check it out bro, this juvi placement you went to doesn't make you look good, plus, you dropping out of high school doesn't help you out at all. You should at least have your high school diploma and you can get it from adult school. And on top of it all, I want to be honest with 'chu, your ASVAB test scores are ass, bro," Cocho could care less how the Marines Corps saw Tierra's incarceration and public education, he wanted top tier recruits that were less of a hassle for himself. And most of all, recruits that boosted his service jacket record.

Tierra has a difficult time processing all of this. Sure, rejection happens in life, but of all places, in a recruiting office for the *warriors* that were known to be the "first to fight and last to leave," they are tripping on an academic test? *Didn't the Marines draft people in Vietnam as long as they were healthy? What standards did they have to reject for the draft, let alone today? Based off whether they passed a stupid test*?

Tierra is beyond frustrated and confused, "You know, I trip out, man. Back in my dad's time during Vietnam when they had that draft shit, they took whoever. Now, they are tripping on my high school diploma and how strong my arithmetic skills are," Tierra let out a scoff that Cocho did not like, but Tierra's frustration got the better of him. Tierra knew like any place trying to sell something, there was always a catch, evidently even in the military when numbers are not desperately needed.

They spoke more to where Cocho exposed his lackluster desire to mentor a troubled youth wanting to change his life, "Look Tierra, you see that uniform right there," Cocho points to the poster of a U.S. Marine in dress blues holding a thin curved sword. The poster shows a clean-shaven man staring whoever looks his way and reads, 'The Few, The Proud, The Marines.'

"That shit sells. I really don't got to do shit or anything for that matter besides drive recruit's around. People come in here and want to be a part of something bigger than themselves, and I mean, look at that uniform, bro. That's why I chose to do this, job," Cocho was building himself up to something he knew was not completely true but sold it anyway. "You have this itch to be something and join something bigger than yourself, right? This is *your calling* to become a Marine. Earn that title, bro."

The Staff Sergeant explains to Tierra that getting his high school diploma from his local adult school could help him by both earning his diploma and brushing up the cobwebs of his arithmetic and mathematics comprehension in general. One way of looking at it, it'd be a win-win, according to the ambitious recruiter. Tierra left the idea of education a long time ago and never planned on going back to high school. He came home defeated. But one of the many things Tierra learned from growing up, giving up is not an option. He had this stubbornness to him that he applied to almost everything who and what he interacted with. Skateboarding in his barrio taught him when you fall off your skateboard five times, you get back up ten more times and continue riding. It was no different with a fist fight. Tierra really thinks about what he should do next, whether to give up and do something else with his life or find some other way to keep "riding" toward his goal. Tierra went to speak with his dad about the exchange.

"You know, when some people ask me what my son is doing, I tell them I am proud, but I also tell them I pray to God, they don't accept you," Guillermo's dad has been saying the same thing ever since Guillermo told him and a few family members about wanting to enlist in the Marine Corps. "Some people think *I am the one* pushing you and convincing you to join. When I went to Vietnam, it was different back then. But the Marines will put your body where they need you," Guillermo's father was completely honest about his own experiences as a Marine himself.

As a Marine whose primary occupation was intelligence, Mauricio volunteered to be a door gunner for the CH-47 Chinook – a long helicopter that always reminded Guillermo of a flying bus with a rear door that flapped open to pick people up. Despite what people thought about who or what influenced him to want to join the Marines, nobody wanted Guill not to join the war machine of the country he defended once upon a time more than his own father.

Guillermo looks at his dad as his father focused on the steering wheel, "I know but I told you I am doing this," Guillermo says firmly.

"That is what I tell people, mijo. I am proud of you so don't think I am not. I don't like it, but I support your choice. You need to understand that it is not easy for me," Mauricio says gently holding in emotions he does not want his son to see.

Guillermo knows his father is being honest with him, which he appreciates. "Well, the news I got today wasn't the greatest. The recruiter is giving me shit because of my ASVAB scores and because I don't have a high school diploma. Not to mention my experience being sent away at that rehabilitation center. Some bullshit, right?"

"Really?! Wow!" Mauricio thought his prayers were being answered. "Things sure have changed from my day. What exactly is wrong with your ASVAB scores and what would you have to do?" Asking, Mauricio hopes that whatever checklist his son had to do would deter him from moving forward.

"Apparently my ASVAB scores are failing. The reading portion seems decent, but my math is shitty. Plus, I've heard from some other guys I met in the Junior Marines that recruiters just want recruits to get the highest score possible so that their quotas and service jacket look that much better. As for my diploma, the Marine Corps requires that you have at least that, but I don't know how true that is," Guillermo thinks he is being lied to, after all, how much education would one need to have to be a jarhead.

Although Mauricio does not want his son to enlist, he knows Guill's mind is made up. "How bad do you want it, Guill? Remember this, from what my dad told me – if you don't do it now, how old will you be when you decide to? You might regret it if you never try," of course, his father was referring to his high school diploma as that would be something Mauricio could get behind and support without regret.

"To be honest, I don't know. I gave up on school a long time ago."

"Come on, Guill, you're talking like if you're my age. You have plenty of time to go back to school and get what you need. Anything you do in life, especially if you want it badly, you will work for it," Mauricio takes occasional glances at his son while maintaining his line of vision returning home on the 60 freeway.

"Thanks, dad. I'll see what I end up doing," Guillermo looks to the window as anxiety creeps.

"As much as I don't want to see you join the Marines from the things I saw, I also don't want you to end up like these assholes I see out in the streets. Eres mejor que eso. ¿Entiendes?" Despite his assimilated background, Guill's father always resorted to Spanish to emphasize the some significance.

"I understand," Guill got out his dad's truck and took his time walking down his apartment driveway as he continues to reflect.

Guill's mom was not home yet in the 2-bedroom apartment in which they live together, so he decides to have some time to himself in the upstairs patio. Retrieving a small, folded penny saver, Guill breaks up some marijuana flower and rolls up a thick cigarette – a personal favorite way of smoking as opposed to using a pipe. He intensely thinks about what his next move should be as he stares at the palm trees that hover over Olympic Boulevard three apartments down. At eighteen with neither a car nor a job, let alone, no income besides breaking into cars and occasional recycling, he knew he couldn't live like this forever. Sure, there were 30- and 40-year-olds who did live like this and although their lives looked "fun" from a surface level, the idea of living without ambition or plans scared Guillermo more than any death or injury that could be inflicted from the hood or military. He spoke to a couple of homeboys he knew he could trust, confided his insecurities to his mother, and a few more conversations with his father. He even took some time to skate at the local park by himself for a week straight. Coming back home one day, he knows what he has to do.

Fuck it… Guillermo decides to attend East Los Angeles Adult School.

CHAPTER FIVE

The East Los Angeles Adult School was located next door to East Los Angeles High off Whittier Boulevard. A small percentage of apprehensive high school students behind credits can be found here working a packet of subjects flunked. The majority of the other students here were single mothers, to-be-fathers working in construction and other blue-collar work, and everyone in between trying to get a job that requires a high school diploma or GED equivalency. Guillermo was among the latter.

Guillermo wakes up early this Monday morning. He serves himself some Frosted Flakes and the cereal tastes different than usual. With every bite he takes, he savors the taste more and more, almost as if his taste buds suddenly enhanced. The feeling of starting a new chapter to get where he wants is imminent and exciting. Getting approved by his recruiter was the goal at hand since it meant Guill has a chance at achieving something with his life. He takes his last bite of the brown crunchy flakes doused with milk and slurps the remaining leftover. He cleans up both his dishes, heads out the door, and takes off on his skateboard down the street known for its palm trees and lowriders. He knows his path to becoming a Marine begins, but first, he must meet with Mrs. Rodriguez.

      The academic counselor at the East Los Angeles Adult School, Mrs. Rodriguez, broke down all the rules and expectations of Guillermo. He had the option to earn his GED or Adult School Diploma, and the recruiter made it specific that Guill should earn his diploma. To complete this, he would have to take U.S. History, Math 1, Math 2, Composition, Reading, Earth Science, and a couple of electives of his choice. Each subject had units he had to completely read and take a quiz at the end of the unit. Each subject differed in how many units he had to read and quiz, but once he completed all units for that subject, Guillermo would have earned 5 credits. Some subjects such as Earth Science required adult school students to read a total of 50 pages, 5 quizzes per 10 pages (or chapters), and the quiz contained about 25 questions, where a 70% or better was needed to move on to the next chapter. Guillermo didn't think too much about the math of it all as it was somewhat overwhelming. To graduate with a high school diploma, a student needed approximately 220 credits and because he dropped out of high school so young, Guill only earned a meager 65 credits while he attended high school in his city. Mrs. Rodriguez said she has seen students earn 5 credits as quickly as 2-3 weeks if they put in the effort. Guillermo always hated math with a romantic passion, but after calculating how long it would take to earn this Adult School Diploma, it would approximately take him 7-8 months to make up the remaining 155 credits.

      And he did. Guillermo would sometimes be offered to be dropped off by his mother at the adult school as she went to work in the same direction, fewer times, he would take his skateboard and ride on his own. When his father was in the area, he would reach out and offer to have lunch. The support Guillermo had from both his parents was immense and it helped tremendously. His parents although divorced and with their own differences have experienced the troubles their son has gone through. They, like most parents wanted their son to thrive, even if it meant the fear of losing him by joining the military. His parents dreaded their only son belonging to the U.S. military, but they also see and know the things that go on in their neighborhood and they both thought, maybe, just maybe, the military might help Guillermo.

The dedication and commitment did surprise his parents as well, but only to some degree, specifically his mother, Sophia. Guillermo loved to argue and question everything, according to his mother. Even at the tender age of eight, just as his mother Sophia was going through a separation with Guillermo's father, young Guill would ask rare questions such as, "Mom, how many stars are there?" and "Who made god?" and "Why are we supposed to believe god is real?" The "Guill, you are just supposed to have faith" never convinced him and he continued to ask "why" after. Questions became much more articulate when he became eleven and asked about one of his closest cousin's fathers who was incarcerated what seemed like forever. Raymond or Ray Ray was Guillermo's closest cousin growing up and unlike Guill's dad who was around most times, Ray Ray's dad, Ignacio was locked up since both morros could barely remember. Ray Ray's mom, Yolanda told her son that on a New Year's Eve, Ignacio got really drunk and shot his gun in the air in celebration and has been incarcerated ever since. By the time Guillermo was eleven, he could not wrap that Ignacio was locked up that long for simply shooting some trigger-happy shots in the air. Guill knew there was jail and prison, and the difference was usually in regard to the severity of a crime. He also knew people spent around a few months to a year or so in jail; where people spent anything longer than that in prison, usually for something much worse.

Sophia encountered Guillermo's insurmountable curiosity, sometimes even obnoxious at times, about his cousin Ray Ray's dad.

"Mom, dad told me the difference between jail and prison. Usually, people stay in jail for stealing stuff or if they get in trouble for the first time. For prison, people go there if they hurt someone or even kill, right?"

Sophia wanted to become a sheriff and was studying criminal justice at East Los Angeles College before Guillermo was born, but the unplanned pregnancy gave her something to look forward to in raising a son instead of enforcing the law. Her son helped in so many ways as he was her only baby boy. Sophia's marriage to Guill's father was extremely difficult and she fell into depression for many years prior to Guill being born. When Guill was born, a new light filled her world of darkness and hopelessness. Her being a bookworm since she was little, Guill picked up the same trait of his mother when he was little – but more than anything, Sophia would always receive compliments from Guill's teachers on how intuitive and articulate her son is. Being much older, Sophia finds it much more difficult to lie to her son for the sake of shielding him from the sometimes-horrific realities parents try so hard to protect their children from.

"Yeah mijo, I believe that's what I learned. Jail can also sometimes be a holding place for bad people while they wait to go to prison too."

Guill knew Ray Ray spoke to his dad every so often on the phone. On some occasions for sleepovers, Guillermo would briefly say hello to his tio. Guillermo didn't think Ignacio sounded like a bad guy and if he was, well, why was Ray Ray allowed to continue talking to his dad?

"So, Ray Ray's dad is a bad person?" Guill asks his mom bluntly.

"What makes you say that, Guill?" Sophia was not

sure where Guill was going with this.

"Well, it doesn't make sense that Ray Ray's dad has been in prison for just shooting a gun in the air," Guillermo's arms were crossed and his eleven-year-old eyes squinted as he focused.

"Mijo, who said he was in prison?"

"Tia told Ray Ray that his dad is in jail. I know that is not true since Ray Ray and me have not seen his dad since we were babies, or at least when I was 3 or 4. His dad has to be in prison and if someone is in prison, he must have done something really bad."

Sophia tried to deter the focus, "You remember people you met or known at 3 years old?"

"Mom, stop. Please tell me, it doesn't make sense. You don't go to jail and stay there for 10 years. I'm eleven and never remember seeing Ray Ray's dad. It sucks that Ray Ray doesn't have his dad home. But I feel that Tia is not being honest, maybe to not hurt Ray Ray's feelings."

Sophia knew she could not lie to Guillermo, but she also knew that it was none of his business. She also understood that Guillermo was mature enough to know the truth, but also knew she didn't have to tell her son why her sister withheld some truth away from Ray Ray.

"Guillermo, I am going to tell you why your cousin's father is incarcerated but you need to swear to me that you will not tell your cousin. It will upset your Tia more than you can imagine and you will gravely hurt your cousin. You love your cousin, right?"

"Of course, mom."

"Then promise me you will never mention what I am going to tell you to your cousin," Sophia emphasized this trust to her son.

"I promise mom. I don't want to hurt my cousin or make Tia angry. I just want to know the truth."

The truth was something Yolanda was planning on

telling Ray Ray when he got older. Ignacio was in a serious relationship with a woman before Yolanda. Ignacio came home to find his partner in bed with another man having an affair. Logic departed faster than the bedroom door that opened and exposed the infidelity at play – Ignacio went for his gun and shot them both dead in bed. Ignacio did not shoot wildly into the air on new year's, and he was certainly not drunk. A crime of passion is what they called it and gave Ignacio a full life sentence. It was during this time that a close girlfriend of Yolanda convinced her to tag along with her to visit a friend in prison and talk to Ignacio. Both Yolanda and Ignacio spoke more, exchanged letters, and eventually exchanged vows and conjugal visits.

Sophia witnessed when Guillermo started experimenting with drugs, getting into fights, and selling weed – he was consistent and appeared to not only indulge but also know what he was doing. Of course, Guillermo did not know the intricate dangers he was getting involved in and his arrogance lead him to his own consequences by his mom intervening with his school by placing him in a juvenile rehabilitation center for at-risk youth. Still, Sophia was impressed by how much energy her son puts into something he focuses on, whether it was his pursuit of knowing the truth about his cousin's father's absence or now working to be accepted by the military. His stubbornness is both a gift and curse.

Sophia knows that he has potential to do something positive and maybe this choice he is making is just that. Guillermo was cranking out 5 credits per week on average. He devoured what he read and was ready to digest more. In one week, Guillermo read 12 units of Literature, an elective of his choice which contained around 8-10 pages per unit, averaging around 100 pages. After each unit, there was a test of 30 questions that consisted of short answers, multiple choice, and true or false. Rather than see it as a grueling and tedious task, he began to see it as his golden ticket to get into the chocolate factory. He grinded and continued to push, and push, and push, and push some more. The young Chicano Sisyphus gladly pushed up his boulder everyday trying to consume material to retain so that he could pass the next test and get closer to getting the number of credits he needed to show the recruiter he is in fact worthy. Guillermo regularly checked in with Mrs. Rodriguez since she was the one who would exchange the tickets once he passed 12 units worth of tests that were well above the minimum grade needed to pass.

Guillermo worked tirelessly every week, Monday through Thursday since Fridays the adult school was closed. He would get there when they opened at 9am and left when they closed down at 8pm. Guillermo was revealing something to himself that would be a profound skill he would later use for the rest of his life – the thought of him knowing how efficient he was at being criminally intelligent, or, "good" at being bad. He truly wanted to see if he could change that direction of energy and is witnessing the changes firsthand! – the skill of tenaciously focusing on tasks to reach a goal. Rather than spending his energy on committing petty, and ephemeral crime, maybe he can actually give his life meaning. He thought of the endless possibilities he could have in the Marine Corps, being this young, a street-smart kid, an anomaly, slowly becoming educated.

The day finally came when Mrs. Rodriguez cheerfully handed him proof of the last 155 credits Guillermo needed before dropping out of high school. "So, how does it feel to earn your high school diploma, Mr. Tierra?" She smiles as she is genuinely excited for him.

"If anyone said I was going to graduate with a diploma as little as a half a year ago, I would have laughed. Other people around me too. It's a trip, really. And I am beyond grateful," Guillermo returns the smile and excitement.

"That's right! And you could have opted for a GED, but you decided to go after your diploma. Also, a misconception, just because you earned your diploma here with us, does not make it any less of a *high school diploma.* If you don't mind me asking Guillermo, what is your next move, college, a specific career you want to pursue? You are so young and have a lot in store for your future," she is eager to know what Guillermo does want to do with his life.

Guillermo explained why he was even there in the first place. Dropping out, finding solace in the streets and doing things teenagers his age do not typically do, going to a juvenile rehab center, and eventually going through the doors of the military recruiting center. Guill felt safe and a genuine comfort from Mrs. Rodriguez. He felt others would surely judge him as a loser or reject of some kind, but not with her, as he opened up quite a bit to her. For Guillermo, she has a particularly sweet and motherly vibe that made him feel cared for.

"Wow, you know, many people come through our doors to complete their education, but many do not come so that they can get into the military like yourself. That takes discipline and dedication. But you must be proud of yourself, Guillermo, your family included as well. I know I certainly am."

"Thank you, Mrs. Rodriguez. It's been a pleasure coming in and talking with you, even if it's for a matter of a few minutes each time," Guillermo and Mrs. Rodriguez finish up and she hands him an honorary document to show the Marine recruiter that Guillermo has earned his diploma along with a transcript of the subjects he completed and in the time he did so.

Guillermo's adult school is approximately a mile and a half away from the recruiting station. The moment he walks out the doors of the adult school, he is imbued with an inexplainable excitement he has never felt before. Guill screams an impressive grito to where two elderly neighbors walking by become startled and shortly upset to see it was a young man doing it for fun. A feeling of immense euphoria that no drug has ever come close to giving this much bliss in the future Marine. He feels a strong sense of pride as he is representing his barrio, his city, his loose identity of a Chicano who is representing his people – he feels he is becoming worthy of something, finally. A feeling that he accomplished something that so many family members and friends doubted he would ever finish. Triumphantly victorious, with papers in his hands, not caring if the wind or his celebratory jumps rendered them bent or crinkled, Guillermo sprints towards the Marine Corps office to show proof that he is not only motivated and driven, but is serious about enlisting.

CHAPTER SIX

B ro, congrats! Fucking A. You sure you didn't cheat or pay someone? Cocho greets Tierra with his own sense of humor and chuckles.

"I did the damn thing. I never thought I'd do it, but every day I worked at it and was seeing the progress unfold," Tierra wipes his face from his forehead to his cheeks as if he just woke up from a dream. "You're lagging it fool! Ship me off to boot already!" Guillermo returns the energy back with his own humor.

Cocho looks through Tierra's papers and did not quite understand some of the transcripts nor how fast Tierra got his credits. "Hey, Tierra, what is this?" Cocho points to U.S. History and the dates he earned the credits.

"Those are credits I earned for U.S. History. To get your credits in adult school, it really depends on each person as to how much time they put in. I was pretty much going all day, every day, getting there when the adult school opened and stayed until it closed," Guillermo explained carefully as he examined the unsatisfactory countenance Cocho maintains.

Cocho looking at the paper points to the testing room of the recruiting office, "Yo, go chill in the study room and review the ASVAB book while I get this checked out with the Gunny. We're going to have to take you to MEPS soon."

Tierra knew that MEPS was the Military Entrance Processing Station where all recruits from all branches get physicals, evaluated, and tested for the official ASVAB. If you went to MEPS, it means you are that much closer to getting shipped off to boot camp. But of course, Cocho said this to distract Tierra so he could further examine the transcripts and check in with his own superior. Frustration to his own illiteracy of not being able to read and comprehend the legible documents that were unofficially declaring Tierra has graduated with a diploma leads the recruiter to make an executive decision. The Staff Sergeant also called the adult school to speak with Mrs. Rodriguez and inquired about the dates and subjects as to how quickly they were earned. Mrs. Rodriguez explains everything to him as if he were a child from the beginning and reassured Tierra earned every single credit legitimately through his own hard work and dedication. Much to Cocho's chagrin, he was not satisfied, and cherry picked a handful of subjects that he felt were earned too quickly. The Staff Sergeant told Mrs. Rodriguez that his recruit needs to redo these subjects.

Cocho calls Tierra back into the main office from the testing room. "I just got off the phone with Mrs. Rodriguez and got some information here. Check it out bro, we both know you are motivated, but these credits look suspect as fuck. Plus, you got some other credits from some juvenile hall place you went to? What's up with that shit on the transcripts, you're getting 'free' credits from that?" The Staff Sergeant did not understand nor cared that Tierra earned elective credits from his stay in his detention center. Mrs. Rodriguez explained this, but it went in one ear of the recruiter and out the other. Tierra looks down with embarrassment as if he did something wrong. The trauma that came with what led to being sent there was not something

Tierra liked talking about.

"They were electives that transferred over. Mrs. Rodriguez said those were legit…" Tierra catches himself from not exploding and did not know what to say as he was blindsided. *How could this be?*

The recruiter stares at the transcript frustrated at his own inability to decipher what "composition" was and how that subject was 20 credits earned in a matter of a month's time.

"Well scope it, I'm going to need you to go back and retake these credits," Cocho shakes his head and points out the subjects composition, U.S. history, physical science, and electives to be retaken.

"Is there a reason why I have to retake these? My adult school counselor who looks over everything and what I needed to graduate has been working with me since the start. Are these not legit?" Tierra becomes concerned as the work he invested is beginning to feel like a waste of time. No, not a waste of time, he busted his ass. Mrs. Rodriguez would not mislead him to a dead end or some cut corner. Tierra's head is in a swirl. But at the same time, it also feels like Cocho is being an asshole, but Tierra needs to play his game.

"To be honest bro, I spoke to my Gunny, and he said these subjects won't fly. You have to retake them," Cocho lies right through his teeth as his superior officer, Gunnery Sergeant Dalisay, gives his recruiters full autonomy to make executive decisions. The more recruits Cocho can record for his quota with higher ASVAB exam scores only helps him. Cocho's own incompetence and pride further block him from appreciating the highly motivated recruit.

"This is some bullshit, Cocho. I worked my ass off to get this done. I don't know how this doesn't show I am trying my hardest to enlist," Guillermo looks straight into the recruiter's eyes.

Defensively and with machismo pride, Cocho shrugs, "Like I said bro, it sucks, but I can only do so much, I don't make the rules. Plus, this is a GED, right? It looks a certain way with low ASVAB scores and your past," Cocho knows he is lying. Cocho also has not come across a recruit with a background such as Tierra and there is something about the potential recruit that he does not like but cannot put his finger on it. It could be Tierra's tenacious attitude that he rarely sees in recruits his age, or it could also be that he envies Tierra's sheer motivation to improve his life as Cocho did the opposite.

Tierra as young as he is, may not be book smart to ace the ASVAB test, but his street intellect can detect when someone is disingenuous. "I had the option to choose GED or an Adult School Diploma, which is equivalent to a high school diploma since you must do all the work on subjects you would take if you attended high school. It's just not in a traditional classroom. I chose the diploma route and that is why I brought the transcripts. Look man, I don't want to waste your time and don't waste mine. I'll talk it over to the Gunny and Mrs. Rodriguez and if I have to redo these credits, then so be it."

Tierra begins to resent Cocho, and his face begins to annoy him to the point where he wants to drive his clenched knuckles directly to his fat light skinned nose. He has the strongest feeling Cocho is wrong, but he cannot prove it. The truth is, this recruiter is the keyholder to crossing the door that Tierra wishes to pass. Tierra has no choice but to go back to East Los Angeles Adult School. And that is just what Tierra does.

CHAPTER SEVEN

Guillermo puts his thinking cap back on and wonders what to do yet again. He ventures back to the East Los Angeles Adult School to explain to Mrs. Rodriguez what his recruiter told him, and it is no easy task for Guill. She listens and he needed just that – someone to simply hear him vent and let out his doubts and worries. The adult school counselor empathized with Guill and encouraged him to rest and think about what he really wants to do from here.

"Guillermo, you put in the work, and it showed. For what it's worth, I do not see too many people working as hard as you did. That shows you are dedicated and more than worthy of achieving your goal to enlist," Mrs. Rodriguez gave a short pause. "I would recommend taking a week or two off, rest and get your head together, and if you wish to come back and retake some of these credits, I will help you every step of the way," Mrs. Rodriguez smiles.

Guill gives his thanks and takes the adult school counselor's advice. He goes to the skatepark for a couple of days to relieve stress and anxiety and alternates other days riding down Whittier Boulevard. On the endless East Los Angeles streets, Guillermo focuses on each crack and curb he jumps over on his skateboard. Skating for hours while listening to shuffled music on his MP3 player, different songs remind him of his past and future, but his present state feels so unrelatable and foreign. He feels alone, somewhat depressed, and defeated, but continues riding on.

One night, almost three weeks of exclusively skateboarding and reflecting, he hangs out on top of his two-story apartment roof that his 74-year-old neighbor Maria screamed at him millions of times to not go up on since he was 13 years old. He looks to the stars, then to Downtown Los Angeles – a gorgeous site of several tall skyscrapers, the U.S. Bank Tower and its siblings, a beacon of home. He stares and thinks about where his life currently is, no job, no higher education, and no career in sight. But wait. He didn't have his high school diploma only months ago and worked for it and earned the damn thing. The very notion of knowing how efficiently "good" he was at being criminal began to click in his mind. That relentless and stubborn energy can in fact be used for something more productive and meaningful, such as earning his high school diploma. So why give up here, now? Fuck that. Things began to suddenly make sense in Guill's mind.

I'll go back, redo these classes, study for the ASVAB, and earn my way in… That asshole can't keep me out if I'm fully legit.

Guillermo went back to speak to Mrs. Rodriguez but this time he switched out his thinking cap with his working one. He went straight back to work, focused, locked in on his target and nothing was going to stop him.

A week after returning back to the adult school, Guill received his actual Adult School Diploma in the mail. A wonderful and rewarding moment that was not celebrated with a graduation ceremony nor party, but it was not needed. Sophia was the first to tell her son, "Estoy muy orgullosa de ti, hijo," and that was more than enough to hear that from his mother. They both went to go eat at both of their favorite Japanese restaurant Taihei in Monterey Park. This piece of paper he worked for shows he could do this, and he continues to remind himself that he will. It is his calling to life to enlist in the service and come back to his barrio and represent not only where he grew up but also show that he could change as a person and make something of his life. Guill wholeheartedly believed this and was going to see this through.

In a month and a half, Guillermo bested yet another obstacle that he first thought would be insurmountable. But Guillermo's mind is as stubborn as his attitude. He has yet again confirmed that his efficiency of indulging in crime can be altered and be just as effective if he focuses on something productive as he is doing now. Today, Guillermo finishes the set of subjects he had to retake because according to his recruiter, they were "earned too quickly." Almost two months ago, rather than foster and acknowledge the effort and hard work put in by the former juvenile delinquent, Tierra was cast close to a cheat. Mrs. Rodriguez protested the recruiter's notion, but did not want to rattle anyone's cage, especially for Guillermo as she knows for him, he has already gone through a lot and knows this means so much for him. This time, it is much different.

"Hello, Guillermo, how are you doing today?" The warmth of Mrs. Rodriguez's smile was no less consistent than the sun rising every day.

"Good, Mrs. Rodriguez, hope you are too, I just don't want my recruiter to find something else that he does not approve and prolong my process to get shipped off to boot camp," Guillermo feels a bit more positive talking to Mrs. Rodriguez even if she could not make magic happen out of thin air.

"Well, I have a feeling your recruiter won't have any problems this time," Mrs. Rodriguez did not tell Guillermo directly, but she purposely spaces out the dates he earned the "questionable credits he earned so fast" according to the Marine recruiter.

"By the way, Guill, there is a writing contest that pays the winner $500 and a chance to be the graduating class valedictorian. The prompt for the contest is, 'why did you attend adult school and what is the significance of education for you?' From what you've told me, I must say, I am quite grabbed by your story. The fact that you had a rough past, came back to school not just for yourself, but for your future is something common here, but uncommon for someone your age as well as the goal you are working towards. Not to mention, coming back here a second time after you finished, most people would have thrown their hands up in the air and just give up. But you didn't. That takes ganas. ¿Entiendes?"

"Si, entiendo, Senora Rodriguez," Guill chuckles as his dad switches to Spanish for the same reason Mrs. Rodriguez does. "As for the contest, I don't know to be honest. I will definitely think about it."

They bid their farewells and Mrs. Rodriguez advises Guillermo not to go to the recruiter right away like he did last time. She wants to make the new transcripts reflect something to what she thinks the recruiter would want to see regarding dates and credits earned by Guillermo. She also wants Guillermo to enter the writing contest for she sees the undeniable drive in him – a story that he needs to share with his graduating class. Surely, Mrs. Rodriguez did have an effect on him as he considered writing his story of what led him to the doors of Mrs. Rodriguez's office, which he is eternally grateful for. If it wasn't for her kindness and support, Guillermo might have in fact just gave up.

A couple of weeks pass and Guill decides to take Mrs. Rodriguez's advice once again by taking some time off from the recruiter's office. It did him some good as he was able to gather and collect himself. He took it easy from skateboarding and began a workout routine like he did when he was incarcerated. And he also decided to try out for the speech contest. So, he wrote, mainly reading out loud to himself and to his mother after she came home from work. After a couple of weeks more, Guillermo folded his 3-page speech and dropped it off to Mrs. Rodriguez's mailbox all the while not expecting to win such a contest. Either way, it was a nice mindful exercise to practice his hand at writing and take his mind off of Cocho and the pressure of enlisting in the Marines.

At times like these – stress, doubt, and worry, would prompt Guillermo to hang out with his homeboys from the neighborhood. But lately, especially since coming out of a juvenile detention center, he did not feel like himself and spent more time alone. A sudden existential struggle for identity has manifested finally from the years of growing up in the barrio. Not being able to speak Spanish fluently with the people around him, only knowing enough to barely get by. The memories of not being able to have conversations with his grandparents, yet still finding some sort of pride in saying "I love you" in the tongue they speak. Living in the barrio and experiencing how las juras pulled over Guillermo and his homeboys many times looking suspicious but doing nothing except walking to the donut shop. Being made fun of for having dark skin with names like "indio, paisa, and mayate," only learning to hate others with the same color skin including himself. Embracing the next-door neighbor's appreciation of both Mexican and American flags dually raised side by side. Seeing both the torture and manipulation of the cholos in our barrio who should ideally look out for the little homies, but instead sell drugs and encourage them to join the gang, and put in work for the hood that will not support them when shit does hit the fan. The fact that Guillermo is leaving his barrio whose gang he has been closely associated with, to leave and join another "barrio" who gangbanged nationally against enemigas foreign, made Guillermo uncertain at times.

Indeed, Guillermo is confused and has never quite felt Mexican, and more so did not feel American. But perhaps within his subconscious, carrying out this purpose of enlisting, he might very well feel like he belongs somewhere. He takes the day off to reflect on top of the roof of his apartment and gaze at the downtown skyscrapers.

The next morning, Guill is woken up by the landline phone.

"Yeah, hello?"

"Good morning, may I speak with Guillermo Tierra?"

"This is him."

"Hello, Guillermo, this is Maritza here at the East Los Angeles Adult School. I hope your morning is going well. I have great news. You are the contest winner for the East LA Adult School Speech Contest! Congratulations!"

Guillermo is a bit stunned and did not know what to think or say right away as he wipes the perspiration off his eyes, "So does this mean I won the $500 prize?"

Maritza chuckled at what was more concerned, "Yes! You also win the 1st place prize that was set. You are also this year's graduating class valedictorian! I know we have not met but I am excited for you!"

"Thank you, that means a lot coming from a stranger. What does the class valedictorian do again?" Guillermo heard the word before but has no idea what such a word does.

"Of course, the speech you wrote, you will present it at the East LA Adult School graduation ceremony. One of our teachers here will sit down with you to help edit your speech as well."

Oh, fuck. Guillermo did not realize he would have to present on top of winning, "Umm, how big is the gradua-

84

tion?"

"Roughly around 200-300 guests in total including adult school graduates and family and friends. But please know that the adult school does encourage you to do the speech as our 1st place winner. If for any reason you cannot, we will have to find someone else to represent our graduating class since 2 other local adult schools will be present."

"No, I'll be there. I just never did a speech before. I dropped out of high school and now I am speaking in front of a big crowd," Guill chuckled nervously and literally thought aloud.

"I understand but I am sure you will be more than fine. Just practice and prepare. I will get one of our teachers here at the center to reach out to you to schedule when you both can edit and work on your speech. Congratulations, again and have a great day!"

The phone call ended. Guill could not believe what was going on. He immediately thinks of what has been in the back of his head for so long now.

Now those fuckers will have to accept me. I mean, shit, I won a speech contest and I'm the class valedictorian representing my city!

As much as Guill wants to call Staff Sergeant Cocho and tell him the news, he wants to wait for Mrs. Rodriguez to give him the green light. Mrs. Rodriguez calls the same day to congratulate and explain the formality of the graduation and duty of the class valedictorian. It was a huge honor to speak for a graduating class and Mrs. Rodriguez emphasizes this to him. She also explains that the transcripts are ready to be taken to the recruiter who made him go back to earn a "second diploma." Guillermo is nervous as another responsibility is on his shoulders, delivering a speech at his own graduation. He slowly works up to the idea that he could speak in front of a large crowd, after all, it would be his graduation on earning an actual high school diploma –

not many of his own homeboys in his own neighborhood could brag about this, not that anyone in the barrio would.

The day came to speak to Cocho again but this time with updated transcripts of redoing work that was not necessary. To add on, Tierra is now the class valedictorian, which was an honor to embrace, especially for a high school dropout. Cocho briefly congratulates Tierra and discusses Tierra's potential MOS's or Military Occupational Specialty, which would be Tierra's job for the next 4 years once he enlists and signs his contract. Things were looking up for Tierra and he felt like things were moving forward. Cocho thinks it'd be best for Tierra to prepare for his speech and at the same time study for the ASVAB test, again. They both agreed and Tierra took off making the interaction purely business instead of seeing Cocho as anything more – he now sees him for who he is, a recruiter.

Part III

CHAPTER EIGHT

Guillermo's graduation was a grand day for him and his family. His half brother from Fresno came all the way down just to attend. A few cousins and a homie from Guill's barrio came through to show their respect. Guillermo composed himself for his speech as class valedictorian and he delivered. He was somewhat surprised it was not as bad as his mind made it out to be – speaking in front of 250-something people. Guill felt on top of the world and he himself was proud of how much he has achieved. But no one could be prouder than both of his parents that saw him going down a path they thought would forever lose their son. The irony of losing their son yet again to a goal set by Guillermo is temporarily put on hold for their son's milestone is what is important for the time being. Even his homeboys from the neighborhood congratulated Guill once they heard the news as even they knew, education was a ticket to doing something productive. Cheers, drinks, and food was had after graduation, and it was a memory Guillermo would not forget anytime soon.

A week later of basking as an adult-school-high-school graduate, Guillermo returns to the recruiting station at 5am. Cocho made plans with Guillermo and another recruit to visit MEPS. This is it. Here is where they process any and all recruits who pass their medical, physical, mental evaluations, and ASVAB tests. Guillermo passes all tests with flying colors, however, the ASVAB once again holds to be an obstacle for him but does not find out until later in the day. The three drive home listening to Barrington Levy's "Black Roses" and Guillermo daydreams of getting shipped off to boot camp. Being yelled at to move with speed and intensity – he knew he was ahead of most recruits from both the experiences of growing up the way he did and completing his stay in the Junior Marines. Cocho receives all documents and results from the MEPS processors via fax in the early afternoon.

"Espinoza, let me talk to Tierra first yeah?" Cocho looks concerned.

The other 18-year-old recruit Espinoza walks into the testing room of the recruiting office. "Damn Tierra, you passed bro!" Cocho smiles at Tierra.

"Really? Fuck! Don't fuck around! You better not be fucking with me! Really?! Holy shit!!" Tierra shouts.

"Yeah bro! Well, look, you passed everything, and did surprisingly well on your mile and half run, 11 pull-ups…you're alright," Guillermo knows Cocho is hiding something.

"You passed the ASVAB too, but you got a low passing ASVAB score. Basically, anything between a score of 39 to 49 is considered BRAVO which is passing, but its average. We want you to get ALPHA tier which is anything 50 or above," Cocho knows that he could accept Tierra in and give him a boot camp date right now, this very day, but he doesn't. Cocho is ahead of his quota and only wants ALPHA scoring recruits to not blemish his outstanding record as recruiter for his station. For every recruit that gets an ALPHA score, it reflects handsomely on the recruiter and his own service jacket record.

Guillermo is livid. "…So, you're telling me I have

to go back to MEPS again, which is all day of mostly doing nothing until they call you and retake the ASVAB again. I've already taken this practice test over 20 times already," Tierra feels every right to be upset. "Bro, I am turning 20 years old, and I just see these 17, 18, year olds getting dates like its popcorn. I took a whole year working on my diploma. I even went back to fix some dumbass credits you thought were not real. That alone should show I'm ready, not this bullshit test score," Tierra chooses his words carefully even though he is extremely upset.

"Tierra, I get you're upset, I'd be too, but I'm trying to help you, bro. Not to mention, I'm still your recruiter and what you say can help or hurt you, I'm just saying," Cocho feels his ego attacked.

Guill becomes triggered, "Fuck that pussy-ass threat, you're not my superior. You can't even get me a fucking date to go to boot camp. You're fucking with me at this point. I busted my fucking ass to attend adult school when I could have been working and earning money. I decided to make sacrifices to prove how serious I was just to get this piece of shit paper. But for what? And now you're telling me to watch how I talk to you? You're full of shit and you know it!" Tierra empties out the gunny sack he was holding inside for the past months.

Just as Tierra finished, Cocho stands up and gets right in Tierra's face. The Gunnery Sergeant, Cocho's supervisor, heard the second half of what Tierra just said to Cocho and walked in the office just as Tierra finished. The Gunny immediately scolds Cocho for standing so close to Tierra and tells him to leave the office to clear his head. The Gunny follows Cocho and they both exchange words, however, Cocho is still heated from the exchange from Tierra who was almost 20 years younger than him. But really, it was his own internal issues with anger and ego that affected the arrogant recruiter. After a few minutes, Gunnery Sergeant Dalisay, a tall Filipino non-commissioned officer with 25-inch arms, returns into the office.

"Look, Tierra, I have been working with Cocho for 2 years now and I am well up to date with your particular scenario," Dalisay clears his throat. "The truth is, right now, you are not fit to join. For whatever reason you have, you cannot get the score on the ASVAB that is best for *us*."

This being the first time Tierra ever really interacted with the Gunny of the office, Tierra is a bit nervous and intimidated. "I just don't understand. I worked really hard to get where I am at. I get I made some decisions in my past that are questionable, but I worked towards making those things right. I proved I am motivated and serious about joining. My transcripts and diploma along with going back to retake credits are proof."

The Gunny held his firm countenance, "You see that picture above in the office? That uniform right there sells itself. People like you want *this*, to be a part of *this*. And you can, but you need to work with us to work with you. You have been very belligerent, and we cannot have that. Whether you join or not, it is not crucial for us, if I can be honest, it won't make a fucking difference as we have plenty of young men like yourself who are more than fit to join our Marine Corps. And that's just the truth of the matter," Tierra heard a very similar pitch before and just realizes who and where it came from.

"So, what do I do now? Just keep studying for this ASVAB test while I get older, while all of these 18-year-old star students walk in here and get dates while I keep waiting?" Tierra still frustrated did not care how his tone sounds.

"Part of the Marine Corps culture is to 'hurry up and wait.' As far as I am concerned, how bad do you want it?" The Gunny recollects himself and fixes the chair he sits on across from Tierra.

"Here is a proposal if you want to speed things up, but it really depends on you on how fast it goes. Go to community college, either East Los Angeles College or Rio Hondo College, since you live in the area, you have either option. Attend, enroll, and complete 15 units. I'm not doing any fucking math, so you figure out how many classes that is. Once you get those 15 units, come back here and not only will that waive this ideal ASVAB score we want you to have, you will also graduate from boot camp as Private First Class, a rank above what most recruits graduate from. You can do that or yeah, keep studying for the ASVAB test while you get older."

Tierra's heart sinks, then it rose to his throat to which he could not swallow back. He just made up 155 credits for his adult school diploma, not his GED. Then he had to retake an additional 35 credits because it appeared "suspicious" to an ego-empowered Marine. Now, Tierra is being told to attend college and take 5 classes worth, 3 units each, to make 15 units. All to satisfy a recruiter's record so that his reputation is maintained, which complements the Gunnery Sergeant's record. Tierra feels his motivation sharply dwindling, the fire that was kindled while in juvenile placement, burned strong during his Junior Marine encampment and pathway to earning his diploma, now, barely surviving by strands, tiny embers on the verge of dying.

"Aight,' Gunny, I'll stay in touch," but of course, what Tierra really wants to say to the Gunny is to go fuck himself.

"You need to understand that earning the title is bigger than yourself. If you need anything, give us a call," an indifferent farewell that is less than half well intended.

CHAPTER NINE

Guillermo breaks the disheartening news with the people closest to him: his parents and Mrs. Rodriguez. They all give uplifting words and encourage him to go to college. Guillermo has no intention or interest in going to college and what annoys him the most is the fact the recruiters know this, along with him being a high school dropout. He thinks the recruiters must have suggested this college idea just to fuck with him and discourage from joining; a bridge he may have burned. Guillermo remembers that the Marine Corps does not need him and that alone hurt him to his core, but this has been set as a life goal ever since his conversation with Zaragosa. In such a dark place surrounded by his own demons from his past, he tries to find the existential rope to climb out of the hell he contributed to creating. At this point in his life, he's too afraid to give up and end up being homeless or without any form of ambition to do or be somebody. Guill wants to do it, despite the news, but doesn't know how. He reminds himself that he wasn't doing this for Zaragosa, or his parents, not even the hood he grew up in; he was doing it for himself, but this speed bump is now becoming a roadblock. Guill also reminds himself that he in fact can put his energy into being productive rather than his usual destructive behavior and did not care if the recruiters wanted him or not. *Me vale madre*. He wants to join for *himself*.

Guillermo's sister, Maya, is attending Rio Hondo College in the city of Whittier. The Gunny was telling this much of truth to Guillermo's options to attend either community college of East Los Angeles College or Rio Hondo, which were in fact in opposite directions but equally far from him. Since his sister is already attending Rio, he decides to go there as she was able to help him with getting acquainted with an academic counselor to set up his educational plan as well as financial aid. Both resources being helpful pieces for any student of lower socioeconomic status attending college.

Guillermo's sister Maya was just over 10 years apart from her brother. The siblings were not estranged but were not close either. Guillermo has memories of Maya taking him everywhere with her friends in the city of East Los Angeles. One time, she dressed up her little brother with brown cowboy boots, a black bandana on his head, and a Harley Davidson shirt, along with a metal chain to hang from his front pocket to his rear pocket jeans. She was a loving older sister to Guillermo and always would be, but her attention was soon given to her own children. Maya also knew of her brother's ambitions to enlist in the Marines, something she was proud of, but deep down, shared the same feelings with their father. She is enthralled to hear her little brother is going to attend the same college as her and hopefully abandon what she thought to be her brother's romanticized ambition to join the military. Naturally, she shows her brother how to make an appointment to see an academic counselor and walks him through the financial aid process which can be a tad bit annoying as there are many nuanced questions of evaluating whether one is in "need" of financial assistance. In Maya's case, since she is older than 24 and lives on her own and makes the amount of money she does, along with Guillermo and their mother's income, according to the financial aid office, they fall into the lower socioeconomic status bracket. Fortunately, for both siblings, financial aid covers most of their expenses.

Taking the bus line 20 on Montebello and Beverly Blvd was not too far as Guillermo rode his skateboard all over the city. Today he was scheduled to meet with James Thomas, his appointed academic counselor that his sister highly suggested as he helped her when she first enrolled to Rio Hondo College.

Guillermo gets on the bus and deposits exactly $2.50 and receives a transfer ticket so he can come back on the same line. The ride to Rio from his city of East LA is roughly 25-30 minutes depending on traffic. Guillermo notices so many things now that he didn't before when riding on the bus. The old and tired faces that never had a childhood by the calices on their fingers and wrinkles on their experienced and working eyes. These older generations of Raza always show Guillermo how hard some people must work and the sacrifices that were made not just for themselves but for their families. He didn't see himself being a father anytime soon, however, that certainly did not mean he did not want to better his life and help those around him such as his family. This relation with seeing these working-class people further reinforces his purpose as to why he was doing this – riding this bus to an institution of higher education that he never, ever, planned to go in the first place. Although he dreads the idea of going to college in fear he may fail, he is reminded of these people that do not have this same privilege he has.

Once the bus passes the 605 freeway that connects the border from north and south Los Angeles, a feint smell of foul sewage permeates the air. One of Southern California's biggest landfills is next door to Rio Hondo College, and as he passes through this infamous area, he confuses the smell with someone who passed vile gas on the bus. Guill's eyebrows are raised as he looks around only to see 66-year-old man as happy as a sunflower in the sun smiling right back at him. Guill shrugs off the grossness of the old man releasing a heinous toxin and continues to look out the bus window. Passing the Rose Hills Cemetery, Guill makes judgmental thoughts about the area of Whittier that he has never been to all that much besides passing. A somewhat industrial and secluded location for a college filled with hills and more hills, railroads, semitrucks, a cemetery, and the smell of shit, but he does not mind, as this is all temporary.

Guillermo is 5 minutes early to meet James Thomas and the academic counselor is called that his 2 o'clock appointment has shown up. Thomas comes out with a straight face and talks to the front desk who takes and makes appointments. Guillermo wasn't sure if the bald, almost 7-foot African American man is his academic counselor, but it looks as though he might be.

"Tierra, Guillermo, is that you, young man?" Thomas is very direct.

Guillermo chuckles to himself as he has not been called that for some time, "Yes, sir, James Thomas, or Dr. Thomas, right?"

"James is fine, youngster. Now how can I help you? Your first time coming to college?" The offices of the counselor were under construction at Rio Hondo College's A-Building, so all appointments were made right outside near the front desk as there are only a handful of computers.

Thomas is a retired Airforce veteran who found education purposefully satisfying. He admires seeing young men and women coming through the doors of higher education not because it gave him a job or something to do, but because he knows the value in what higher education can do for people. Especially for people of color. Thomas, being in his early 50s, looks as though he is barely pushing 40, but the way that he speaks with confidence and bluntness, Guillermo immediately recognizes he wasn't some college square. No, Guillermo knows he's been around the block more than once. To people in the barrio, Thomas would be known as an OG – someone who was much older, who had a lot of life experience, and was rightfully respected. Not only was Thomas honorably discharged from the military, but he also went to college, graduated, and earned his Ph.D., and then decided to become an academic counselor and professor to mentor students in what he loves to see them doing, matriculating. OG shit Guill could sense, and he respected that.

"Yeah, it's my first time. I am trying to get into the Marine Corps," Guillermo feels proud saying what his plan is.

Thomas gives Guillermo a very peculiar look, "And just how is coming to college going to help you become a faithful jarhead?"

Guill could see that Thomas knows quite a bit, including nuanced terms of the military. "It's a long story, but the short version is by coming here and receiving 15 transferable units, I'll get promoted to PFC," Guillermo left out his juvenile detention center experience, the failed ASVAB exams, and especially the friction he has going on with his recruiter.

"Well look at it as *earning* rather than 'receiving,' since you will be earning everything in the Corps. I know a bit since I was in the military myself, the Airforce, twenty years. Did my time and let Uncle Sam pay for my education and now I am here doing what I absolutely love, helping youngsters like yourself," Thomas looks right into Guillermo's eyes, straight to the point and forthcoming.

"What a trip. Well, thank you for your service,"

Guillermo did not know what more to say but is grateful for the directness of his academic counselor and got a good vibe from him, a very different vibe from his own recruiter.

"Don't thank me just yet," Thomas chuckles. "You in a relationship, gotta' girl supporting you in all that you're doing?"

The comical bluntness of Thomas catches Guillermo off guard. Guill looks around to see if anyone heard Thomas ask something he thought was somewhat personal between strangers. "Umm, something like that, why the question?" Guill is not tied down to any relationships at the time but was talking to a girl that he did not give any time to for his own selfish reasons with the military.

"Not anymore you don't! I am going to set you up with 4 classes, but you'll have the option of taking a sociology or Chicano studies class for your fourth, and that will mean you are full-time status. You're going to be too busy to be talking to any girls," Thomas smiles. "You also got a class with me from those 4. From the appointment you made, it looks like you are already set up with your financial aid, so you're set. Welcome to college, young man."

The college-thing is happening so fast, and Guillermo appreciates a challenge, but these are uncharted waters. Not to mention the first person helping him as his academic counselor and future professor is African American, to where he was expecting a white man. Guillermo did not feel he is racist, unaware of what implicit bias is, however, he had no exposure of being around other ethnicities besides Raza and Asian. Still, Guillermo finds some peculiar comfort being helped by Thomas instead of a white man and could not explain how or why.

"Sounds good James, thank you for helping me out with all of this. And these 4 classes will get me my 15 transferable units I need for the Marines, right?" Guillermo is that much more focused on getting the units he needs so he can get shipped off to boot camp.

"Not necessarily. You will have 12 transferable units and that is if you pass all 4 classes with a C grade or better," Guillermo could not help but feel a bit of trauma from what feels like his intelligence is being measured, yet again.

"I am setting you up with 12 units worth of classes because it is your first time and don't want you to get over-whelmed. Not saying you will get overwhelmed, but I been doing this for many years. You can take one 3-unit class over the summer after this Spring semester and that will get you your 15 transferable units your recruiters need. If the Marines is what you are aiming for, I will help you, but you got to help yourself by doing your best in college too."

Fuck...Guill looks a bit disappointed he would not finish the "necessary" 15 transferable units in one semester that the recruiter suggested, and Thomas notices it.

"Guillermo, the fact that you want to join the military is a big commitment. Don't let taking some classes over a small period of time hold you back. You'll be just fine. Just work hard, ask plenty of questions, and keep your eyes on the prize. I see a fire in you that you want this, and you will get to it, but you also have to believe it too. Have patience, you can do this," Thomas means every word. The academic counselor is committed to seeing his students do well in college and eventually graduate and he knows the pep talks helps.

"Thanks, James. When are your office hours?" Guillermo's almost diminished hope is held by mere strands of empathy by a complete stranger.

"Let's walk to these computers over here so we can make your classes official. And here are my office hours, Guillermo," Thomas places his hand over Guill's back and walks him over to show him how to look up classes and add them to his schedule. For the first time, Guillermo has a mentor outside of his family that genuinely cares about his decision.

CHAPTER TEN

The spring semester is not the typical time a new student starts college and there are usually less classes offered in the spring, since the fall semester is the busiest. The first class on his schedule is an entry level English course taught by Professor Gavin – a white middle-aged man with short and curly dirty blonde hair and round belly complemented with a t-shirt and blue jeans. Guillermo's first thought is he could pass for a Santa Claus at the shopping mall if he wore the appropriate fitting. The class is quiet, and Guillermo did not know what to expect. The first things Professor Gavin wants is for everyone to introduce themselves on the first day.

"Okay, good morning, everyone! Welcome to English 35, I am Professor Gavin. I've been here at Rio Hondo for a little over two decades now. For the first day we will go over the syllabus and conduct introductions and how the class will run. We will go around the class and share with each other three things: your name, your year in college, and your major," the professor's voice was quite monotone and simple.

Everyone around shares how it is mostly everyone's first or second year in college. Some majors Guillermo hears are nursing, business, and mostly undecided. Guillermo doesn't have a major in mind and doesn't really know what he would major in if he was going to college for a degree. His mother used to always jokingly tell him that if he ever went to college, that he would love philosophy since his mind asked unusual questions at such a young age. Philosophical questions that always made his mother, Sophia, raise an eyebrow. *Who created god? How do we know what exactly happens when we die? You're going to live for a really long time, right?* Perhaps an existential fear toddler Guillermo would ponder. Growing up in his neighborhood, he never heard other homies talk about the future, or contemplate goals, for when such a topic of a similar nature came up, it was deemed "gay." So, Guill learned to suppress the natural element in us all to question life where things that cannot be answered simply by religious dogmas.

The next person to share with the class is Guillermo. He does not care for impressing his professors or getting perfect scores on anything. He just wants to pass his classes and go to boot camp. He notices that all his classmates of about 25 students all look at his direction causing him to clear his throat before speaking, "Hello everyone. My name is Guillermo Tierra, but please call me Guill. This is my first year and first semester in college, actually. My major in mind right now is philosophy. Maybe writing or English, maybe both. Yeah, I think both, but I'm not sure," of course, Guill left out the Marine Corps for not knowing if others would make fun of him or not understand his choice.

At that moment, Professor Gavin interjects with a scoff before saying, "How noble of you to such majors," the professor laughs and contagiousness spreads to a handful of other students, however not everyone laughs.

Guillermo laughs with them, so he did not seem offended which he somewhat did. *Why would these majors be "noble?" The fuck is his problem?* This is the first real interaction Guillermo has with a professor and for the first time in a long time, he feels insulted to where he did not know what to say back or do. If this was his street, he could simply cap some derogatory slur back, but these unfamiliar grounds suspend him from any action or words. So, Guillermo continues to laugh until the laughing stops and moves on to the next student. He doesn't talk to any of his classmates, nor does he ask the professor for clarification if anything is confusing or unclear – he just does what he is told.

The English, reading, academic counseling, and Chicano studies classes are his current mission and if Guillermo has any notion to join the Marine Corps, he needs to do well in all four of these courses. This means going along with pompous behaviors – something very new and obnoxious to Guill. Participation in all these classes was encouraged but not required, which worked well since he wishes to fly under the radar. At times when he would walk from one class to another in his small college campus, it felt as if this was Guill's second chance at high school. The same positive results he saw in adult school, all that energy he invested in, he was doing the same with all of his college classes. He was maintaining a balance with his work and felt he was treading the running waters of the college student, decently. But from this revelation of his experience attending college for the first time at twenty years old, nothing hit harder than his Chicano Studies class.

CHAPTER ELEVEN

Professor Martinez is a dark complected Chicano. His eyes are walnut shaped, and he carries a particular energy about him that is inviting. It could also be that he looks relatively young for a professor, but then again, those notions or prejudgments might be stereotypes of what Guillermo imagines. It might have also been the fact that this was not a white professor like Gavin – having representation is inspiring for Guillermo as he suspects just about anyone who held a title of professor would be white. But this is not an ivy league institution and Guillermo was learning all the sorts of politics that exist not just outside of the higher educational institution, but in fact within these walls as well.

"Can anyone tell me who are the majority of students coming to college? Ethnicity-wise, specifically?" Professor Martinez opens with this question on the first day of the semester.

An apprehensive classmate to Guillermo's left raises her hand and is called on. "People of color, no?"

"Very good, yes. And your name is? And what specific group of people of color?" Professor Martinez replies gladly and learns one of his new student's names.

Another student raises his hand and tries his answer,

"Mexicans."

"Let's try the word, Raza," Professor Martinez slows his response. "For far too long, the group of what we know as Hispanics or Latinos make up the largest group of ethnicities attending college. I simply choose and prefer the word, Raza, and we will certainly go over these terms later in the semester as well. Our Raza is the largest group of ethnicities going to college and many find it something to be proud of," Professor Martinez pauses and walks to the opposite side of the classroom while looking to the floor before raising his gaze to his audience. "Now, can anyone tell me who biggest student ethnic group that drops out of college?"

Guillermo really thinks he knows the answer and wants to raise his hand.

It's got to be white folks, right? I mean why would "Raza" be the largest ethnic group to attend college and the largest group to drop out of college…?

Before coming to the realization that this in fact can be true, Professor Martinez gives the answer rather quicker, unlike the former question. Nodding his head, the professor's face becomes quite serious.

"Although there are more of our people, or Raza, for those that may not identify as Raza or are a different ethnicity in this class, there are more Raza attending and dropping out of college. Less than 3% of our people graduate with a master's degree," Professor Martinez looks around the class as he pauses.

"But Professor Martinez, what about an associate degree and bachelor's degree?" The professor pretends to be a student asking himself a rhetorical question he is too familiar with.

"Well, the thing is folks, today, a decade after the millennium, a bachelor's degree is weighed equivalent to a high school diploma," a few of Guillermo's classmates scoff and a few others lightly gasp. Guillermo feels upset to hear this from the work he had to do just to get an adult school diploma, alone.

A student raises her hand and asks, "Profe, but what if the job you want only requires an associate or a bachelors, even a high school diploma? Would it really make a difference to go beyond what you need at that point? Especially if it is something you really enjoy and don't need more education after a certain point?" The student's question is genuine and appreciated.

"Excellent question! What was your name?" The professor inquires.

"Martha," the now nervous student that has the attention of both the professor and her classmates answers somewhat faintly.

"Before I answer your question, Martha, I'd like to share a bedtime story told to me by my grandmother, if that would be okay with you and the class," Professor Martinez looks to his audience for approval, but of course looks to get the approval from Martha, first. Martha smiles and nods her head while the class anticipates what the professor has to share.

"Okay, let's see if I recall this. Y'all have heard of the Mexica People known as the Aztecs, right? And I am saying that correctly – Meh-Shee-Ka. The Mexica People, your ancestors were amazingly intelligent people, not the barbarians that sacrificed every chance they got like some ignorant people say and inaccurate movies show. Not only were they intelligent people, but they were also highly philosophical and spiritual. They had many worldviews but one that is strong I personally think you all would appreciate is of *teotl* – our ancestors believed this *teotl* as a type of divine energy that permeated everything, the grass, the sky, the very Earth you walk on. This may sound familiar to some Star Wars fans here. It really reminds me of the

113

'Force,' and like the Force, it is found in everything – an energy if you will, that moves everything and is in everything, including ourselves," Professor Martinez stops to smile and receives a few laughs from those fans that understand what he meant, including Guillermo.

"But remember folks, our ancestors had this philosophical concept long before George Lucas," Professor Martinez has his audience's complete attention. "Now, this concept of *teotl* can also be interpreted on the importance of fulfilling a person's role in the cosmic order and anything less of fulfilling one's purpose was believed to disturb the harmonious balance that is the universe we inhabit."

Martha and some students looked confused. Some student muttered, "Profe, what does this have to do with college or a degree? I'm lost, what's going on?"

"Now don't worry, I haven't forgot about the bedtime story from mi Abuela... I want you all to try to imagine a young Aztec warrior named Cualli. Cualli was earning his rank to become a great Eagle Warrior, the highest-ranking warrior in what you can imagine the Mexica military to be," Guillermo is already absorbed in by the professor's opening lecture but even more so now with history of what would be his ancestors' military.

Professor Martinez continues, "Cualli in the beginning struggled with his path to becoming an eagle warrior with rigorous training, hunting, learning of strategic warfare, and capturing captives for ceremonial practices. Along the way, Cualli was tempted by a more laxed path by a few friends in his circle, finding shortcuts and doing the bare minimum. However, the god Huitzilopochtli, got wind of what Cualli was doing and appeared to him as a manifestation in a dream. The god reminded Cualli of his duty to his people and the meaning behind earning his rank as Eagle Warrior. Huitzilopochtli helped Cualli by showing the challenges and obstacles that lay ahead, consequences as well, if Caulli continues to not work hard like his friends. Cualli realized that to overcome his own challenges, including those of doing the bare minimum, he must embrace the arduous path and work tirelessly to hone his skills if he is to rightfully earn his rank as an Eagle Warrior. Surely enough, the day came where Cualli and his friends were to kill and bring back a jaguar to prove they are worthy. Inspired by the divine message from Huitzilopochtli, Cualli was thoroughly prepared and accomplished his task by capturing a jaguar to where his friends perished by the claws and teeth of the very beast," the professor finishes his story.

"Now, mi Abuela told that story much better," the professor looks up to the ceiling but quickly comes back. "What do you think the moral of my Abuela's bedtime story was?" He asks.

Martha raises her hand as she along with everyone else paid close attention, "The moral of the story seems to be that if you cut corners, it'll catch up to you someday. You got to work hard and put the effort in or in the end, you might not be prepared."

"That is an excellent interpretation, Martha, I couldn't have said it better. And, so, to answer your question, yes, it does make a significant difference. Having a college degree even though you may not need it can greatly help you. Sure, having a decent paying salary can provide you with additional opportunities like buying a car and home, but sharpening your skill to be a critical thinker – just about all jobs look for individuals that possess such a skill as it is something many people lack," Professor Martinez smiles.

"Think about how the velocity of an arrow that is shot at a target from a distance," the professor moves to the opposite side of the room while holding an invisible bow with his left hand and nock of an arrow on his right. "The arrow once shot, because of gravity, will eventually be pulled down by the laws of physics from the force behind the bow that was drawn and let loose," holding the invisible arrow, the professor holds the arrow in midflight walking fast to an imaginary target lowering the arrow as he walks across the other side of the room.

"For many of us, we want to do the bare minimum. And when we aim for that target dead center by ignoring the 'laws of physics' – consequences, procrastination, the who-gives-a-shit-I-will-most-likely-never-have-to-take-this-class-again-for-the-rest-of-my-life – what do you think happens when your effort, i.e. the arrow reaches your goal, i.e. the target?" This time many students raise their hands.

Yes, your name," the professor points to Guillermo.

"Guillermo, Profe. Not being aware of where we are aiming from with no practice or preparation will make the arrow drop low missing the target all together. You need to aim higher," Guill answers.

"What is your name, again?" Professor Martinez asks.

"Guillermo, Profe."

"Thank you, Guillermo for answering, and yes! Velocity of the arrow will drop from a distance, even if you have your sights on the center of that target. Because of that, aim high with focus and awareness and not just for our class, but all of your classes. And not just classes here in college, but apply it to life in general," most of the students appreciate the meaning behind the metaphor and are that much drawn in to the professor's colorful mind.

"Now, we still have to get through the syllabus and introduce each other so let's see how many of us can get that done today and we'll finish the rest next time," the professor's enthusiasm was authentic, and Guillermo could listen to him speak all day.

CHAPTER TWELVE

Professor Martinez's Chicano Studies class is Guillermo's favorite by far. The foreign routine of going over readings, transmitting ideas onto paper, and sharing what each of Guillermo's classmates experienced from the assignments, stimulates him to see how engaging reading can be when it is a subject that is actually interesting. Reading about untaught topics from his public-school education system keeps Guillermo hungry to digest more about his history and ancestors. Guillermo is surprised to learn that the word "Chicano" was a derogatory word that insulted Mexican Americans prior to the Civil Rights Movement by both Mexicanos and whites from the United States – but mainly by the binds of colonialism.

The invading attack of colonization by the Spanish came in 1521 – the invaders destroyed books, culture, and the very fabric of the Mexica People. This untold history was both disturbing and fascinating for Guill. In addition to never learning this history in school, nobody ever taught him about how the Mexica (commonly known as the Aztecs) People were victorious over the European invaders and celebrated the victory known as La Noche de Victoria – known as La Noche de Triste for the Spanish invaders. Of course, history has written that the Spanish not only were victorious, but they also "helped save" the Mexica People from their savage ways and brought "civilization" to them. Guill also learns that the Spanish were actually victorious of their conquest by colluding with neighboring tribes, their technology, cowardice, and diseases they brought. These unpopular parts of history are what ultimately led to the fall of Tenochtitlán – the capital of the Mexica People.

In the same token, no teacher or curriculum went over the amazing accomplishments of Mesoamerican people in Guill's time in public school either. The vast accomplishments of his ancestors that charted the stars, engineered complex aqueduct systems, harvested intricate agricultural systems for an entire civilization, built amazing architecture for a variety of purposes, and created beautiful flower and songs known as poetry – a new world was presented to Guill he did not know existed of the past. And Professor Martinez explained there are reasons why so many of his own students do not know about these things either: assimilation. And the professor was careful on how he explained the matter on the public American educational system, today.

Sure, American schools go over the Native Americans and some of their accomplishments, but a rather inaccurate picture, as Natives and pilgrims "did not break bread on the same table." This, in a class discussion of Guill's, went on to discuss why these parts of history are fabricated and "whitewashed." Many concluded on their own, the reasons why these things are taught, are for people to not question the cruelty of this country and promote a sense of national pride of being an *American*. But the Profe asks his class, "What does an *American* mean? And who specifically were the liberties and rights intended for?" These types of questions and discussions intrigued Guillermo. He felt a new part of his mind working – a way of thinking about society, his place, and others around him in it. But history did not stop there, regarding the Native People of this country. He also learns about a concept called, Manifest Destiny, and how it led to the stealing, murdering, and genocide of the Native American people from this so-called country. All the while learning about these things, Guill could not help but wonder what side the Marine Corps would fall on within these histories of this country. In other words, would the Marine Corps justify all these actions the United States committed? Would the Marines today side with assimilation and nationality of this country? Guill constantly wrestled with these thoughts.

In addition to learning about the involvement of the United States of America in a different light, Guillermo could not believe that California, Nevada, Arizona, Utah, and several more states used to be a part of Mexico. However, Professor Martinez is careful to point out that although these states belonged to Mexico before the U.S., there were Indigenous People that have occupied it long before any country could claim it. The history of his ancestors, their accomplishments, intellect, philosophical and spiritual ways before the Spanish invaded, gave Guill a sense of pride he did not know nor feel before. Guill never saw Aztecs or the Mexica People to have been intelligent, let alone impressive, but he was learning things that he never learned in his schooling before and a lot of it was due to the act and practice of colonialism that still goes on today. Connecting the dots became a revelation for Guillermo as there were so many connections he was making from the past to the present day that he sees what influences himself and the people around him.

Perhaps the most revealing of history Guillermo learns from his Chicano Studies class was the Bracero Program. Guillermo never knew the difference of the connotations between "immigrant" and "illegal," nor did he ever learn about the U.S. program that allowed immigrants to conveniently come to the U.S. to help the very country that stole from theirs. Apparently, the U.S. needed more help from people outside the country since many men and women within the U.S. were working and taking on different responsibilities that the country required of them during WWII. Guillermo did think on his own how contradictory this was – *why are Mexicans and immigrants casted as such a plague by this country, even today?* Even some of Guill's own family shared this castigation of Mexicans and immigrants, which confused Guill as to why his own family of Mexican descent would take this worldview? Assimilation – *what is this? ...Holy fuck...*

It feels very hypocritical to Guillermo, even hurts a little bit, a stabbing feeling in the gut of what he was being taught by family, friends, and society as a whole. He did not want to share his thoughts with the class because he was just there to take the class and pass, but he could not help but feel betrayed by this country and what it sells for image and money: supposed freedom.

Professor Martinez is always careful not to let his bias be too revealed to his class, although it does bleed out from time to time, he does a great job letting his students think for themselves. Guillermo feels a new sense of passion to want to learn more about the topics Professor Martinez lectured. The more he learned, the more Guill became surprised by how it all made him reflect about himself within the world.

One day, one of Guillermo's classmates, Ruben, raises his hand and genuinely asks, "¿Profe, por que las escuelas aquí no enseñan esta historia de los Estados Unidos?"

"¿Naciste aquí? If you don't mind me asking?" Professor Martinez steps a bit closer to the student with curiosity.

"Si, aquí, pero my family and I talked about this

before how so much of U.S. history is taught differently. They don't teach these things like the Bracero Program or the genocide of this country in elementary or middle school."

"Yeah, that is true, after all, educational systems will vary depending on the country. Well, Ruben, I don't always like answering a question with a question, but let's all think about some potential answers to your question, because there might be more than one," Professor Martinez invites everyone to think.

Another classmate, Luis, raises his hand, "Because the U.S. is evil," the class laughs.

Professor Martinez slightly wiggles his head from side to side to not disagree, "Well let's say a little more than describe the U.S.'s empirical nature," the class laugh together again.

Guillermo decided to raise his hand for the second time after weeks of not speaking, "I am not sure, but racism? It is ironic that I learned about the pilgrims and Native Americans breaking bread and eating turkey together on the same table but leave out all the shit the U.S. committed against the Native People, including stealing all their land."

"Thank you, Guillermo, and good answer. I think you, and all of us are helping each other understand this better as to why the U.S. may not want to teach this to our public school system. We are perhaps getting closer. And what may be a cause of this racism from what Guillermo mentioned in the beginning?"

Guillermo feels good participating in discussion even if it is to be short-lived. He feels a sense of community and pride for speaking up, as it not only terrifies him but also excites him as college is not as intimidating and exclusive as he first saw it to be just a couple of months ago.

Another one of Guillermo's classmates, Cassandra raises her hand, "How about colonization? From what

Guillermo said, colonization can be a cause of racism. Racism is not only white attacking Black or Brown, but it can also be taught to our people. We enact racism on our people just about every day as well, which of course comes from the systemic racism that colonization spawned, and colonialism continues. So, it may be why the U.S. does not want to teach the 'truth' about the dark history of this country and its secrets, to promote a type of nationalism and sweep the effects of colonization under the rug. Either that or teaching about that violence is simply too disturbing for young kids."

Professor Martinez smiles and gently nods his head. It is students and conversations like such that keep him coming back to continue teaching students these elements of critical thinking and culture. "Well done, Cassandra. As we approach the end of our lecture, which I know is getting good, we will cover what exactly nationalism is by watching a Twilight Zone episode called 'He's Alive,' and why should we even be aware of such an ideology."

CHAPTER THIRTEEN

The midterm season comes around the corner and Guillermo continues to focus on his classes and work out for the Marine Corps, but the one class he actually looks forward to is Professor Martinez's Chicano Studies. Today's midterm falls on a very calm Thursday. Just outside of Professor Martinez's class is one of many scenic views from Rio Hondo College of the San Gabriel Valley. Rio Hondo College being on top of a large hill, surrounded by natural preserve, makes it a very peaceful spot to be alone, even if it is just 15 minutes to wait for a class to start. Martinez's midterm for his students gives the option of 3 separate prompts to write a timed essay from the history and culture covered in class. Professor Martinez comes to class and his demeanor is a bit unusual. He usually smiles and greets his students at the start of class, but today he does not. His countenance also looks as though he is defeated, and Guillermo thinks it to be somewhat alarming since he has never encountered such a sight from his other professors this semester, let alone, former school teachers. Professor Martinez passes out the prompts for his class to choose individually and gives instructions.

"Okay folks, before we begin, I have to be honest. I am not feeling the best right now. As a matter of fact, I feel quite down, depressed actually. The only reason I am sharing this with you all is because you are my students, and I just want to share how I am feeling today. As for the midterm, do your best, you can only use class notes, no phones or laptops should be out as we already went over this last week. You will have the entire class to finish your midterm. Good luck to you all," Professor Martinez always seems cheerful, but it was somewhat disturbing to Guillermo to see this much vulnerability come out of a person with the title of a college professor.

The prompts were simple for Guillermo as he readily prepared for this exam. He could answer any of the 3 if he wanted but decides to tackle the prompt:

"What is the American Dream and does it exist? For who? And why?"

Guillermo went straight to work and got to 4 pages with time to spare before class ended. There was still 25 minutes left of class and he could leave early now that he had just finished, but he waits. Guillermo wants to share something with Professor Martinez from what he told the class before the midterm. Guillermo wants this to be as private as possible, so he waits for more of his classmates to turn in their essays before he turns his in. Another 10 minutes go by and Guill is 3rd to the last student in class. The other two students he rarely sees in class so doesn't mind if they hear what he has to say.

"Here you are, Profe," Guill hands the handwritten essay in.

"Thank you, Guillermo, have a good day and see you next week," the professor kindly says.

"Well actually, I wanted to share some stuff with you and hopefully it's not weird," Guill thinks about the inferior judgements he would receive in his neighborhood if he shared what he is about to.

"I went through depression myself. Anxiety too.

And I am sure you know that both things never really go away, the symptoms just sometimes subside. Living in my barrio and doing the mamadas I did, didn't help me much either," Guillermo chuckles as he never really shared his past with anyone, let alone a college professor he barely knows.

"My mom was concerned for me, so with her basic insurance, she was able to get me a therapist. I went to therapy and saw at least 4 psychiatrists, which those fucks basically made me feel like a fucking guinea pig, excuse my French. I was on Zoloft, Prozac, Lexapro, shit, one of them fuckers must have thought it would be funny for me to get on Ritalin," Professor Martinez can appreciate the dark humor by his empathetic student and releases a subtle chuckle.

"But yeah, Profe, none of those meds really helped me. Then again, I wasn't consistent as I found some peace being outside in the streets and getting into more trouble. Once I got my head out of my ass, I found that working out, going running as well as walking daily helped me. Oddly, even thinking positive helped me, although I still have trouble with it to this day. See, where I grew up, I used to do some bad things that lead me to a center for troubled teens," it sounded weird to Guill calling himself a term he always heard from those working in these facilities.

"I learned a lot while inside and one of those things is you can't rely on one thing, like medication or even a community – most times, it's drawing strength from within ourselves. Excuse my French again, Profe, but that shit is fucking hard and I'm still learning that. So, I think that can help you, by focusing on the good in your life and working out and getting outside as much as you can. One thing I want to share is that you truly made me think about my culture and identity as a Chicano – I actually look forward coming to your class everyday and I'm not just saying that."

Professor Martinez was stunned by what came out of Guillermo since he rarely spoke out in class. Guillermo to the professor looked no older than 18- or 19-years young. Not to mention the emphasis that this is the most he has ever heard Guillermo speak in his class besides a comment or two, or question to clarify. But more than stunned, Professor Martinez was touched by this genuine act of kindness.

"…I-I'm not sure what to say, Guillermo. Thank you for shar-Wait, how old are you if you don't mind me asking?"

"I am turning 21 this year."

"And what is your major, plans after college? Again, if you don't mind sharing that?" The professor fixes himself on his chair to get more comfortable.

Guillermo reassures him there is no problem with the questions and explains the entire scenario of what lead him from juvenile rehabilitation center to the Marine Corps recruiting office, adult school, the back and forth, and now college.

"Wow, that is a lot. And you're only 20. You know my dad was in the Marines too…"

"Mine too!" Guillermo laughs.

"Well, the point I want to make is, have you thought about finishing your college up and getting your bachelor's degree? You know you can try out to be an officer in the military as that will give you more money and more opportunities," Professor Martinez could not stand the idea someone so intelligent and articulate wanting to throw his life away to the war machine that is the U.S.

"But that's right…You just need the 15 units to get in and you've been working pretty hard to get in as of late. You probably already have a job in mind to go in as enlisted," Professor Martinez wanted to shake Guillermo by his shoulders and scream bloody murder into his face that it was the wrong idea, to run far, far away from any military recruiter. But as a professor and fellow human, a proud Chicano who wants to see his people thrive, he knew he should allow Guillermo to figure out his own path.

"I really appreciate your teaching Profe, I do. Even though I am only here for a semester and a summer to get my 15 units, I'd lie if I were to say that your class is not my favorite. The stuff I am learning in your class has been revealing and you do it with passion and care. As a matter of fact, your class and not only what you teach, but how you go about it has made me reflect on my decision. I never thought I'd have a Profe as firme as you as I thought all professors in college would be gabachos," Guill lets out a chuckle that is contagious for Martinez.

"I feel comfortable in your class, and you explain material to us where I don't feel stupid like other teachers. That is something you should be aware of, that you make a difference with teaching. And I am sure I am not the only one," Professor Martinez appreciates the kindness coming from Guillermo.

"I really appreciate that, Guillermo. But back to the military thing. I've never told anyone what to do, especially my students whenever a private, rare-ish talk like this happens. But I really suggest you give college a chance, not to avoid the military, still go since that is your goal, but go with a college degree," The professor thinks that if Guillermo gives college a chance, hopefully he might find something more bountiful and fulfilling than the military.

"You are wise for your age, and I see such grand potential in you. Have you considered even teaching? Ah! That's it! That is exactly what I can see. The way you carry yourself and determination in your eyes…" The professor sees a bit of himself in Guillermo.

Guillermo never really took compliments, at least

not from anyone besides his parents, but it has been some time since someone had praised him besides Mrs. Rodriguez from the adult school and accepted it. "I appreciate that, Profe, I really do. But I never saw myself teaching, let alone coming to college. Matter of fact, college was never on my list of things to do, but here I am. I am surprised I am here to begin with, and by the motivations to why I am here, but for that reason, it shows me how much I want this and the work I am putting in to get to where I want to be, you know."

"Oh, there is no doubt about that, Guillermo. You are working hard, and the effort shows. But I have to say, your determination, the way you spoke to me not only with empathy but also with care, the effort you have put in class in your writing as well…excuse me for saying this and please do not take offense by this, you are too intelligent to enlist in the Marine Corps. I mean well by saying that. But if you still choose to enlist, please do consider graduating from a university with your bachelor's degree. That way you not only have more opportunities but can enlist into OCS and perhaps become an officer in the military," Professor Martinez meant what he said but not so much the latter portion of Guillermo becoming an officer.

"Thanks again. I'll keep this in mind," Guillermo has a lot to carry out from the midterm to think about and it wasn't about whether he did well on the exam or not.

"Enjoy the rest of your week, Guillermo. And thank you for speaking to me and giving me some advice," Professor Martinez waved.

This was something for Guillermo to think about and consider. Going to Officer Candidate School would mean he would make more money and have more opportunities, but of course, this meant that he would have to stay in college for a few more years before reaching his goal to obtain the title of Marine.

There was a seed that was planted in Guillermo's head, and it began sprouting from the day he figured out that he was excellent at being mischievous and criminal and changing the trajectory of that energy to something productive. His accomplishments of completing his 2-week encampment in the Junior Marines, earning his Adult School Diploma and returning to redo credits, winning a speech contest that led him to speak as his graduating class valedictorian, and now here in college and doing well – all this energy and work is going towards his goals. Nothing else in the world could show Guillermo more that he was a hardworking individual. The gratitude and acknowledgement that came from both Mrs. Rodriguez and Professor Martinez also made Guillermo think if the Marine Corps may not be his calling in life like he believed in the recent years of his early adult life.

Does the military need more people? People like me. Chicanos? Is our country even in danger? Or is the U.S. military a danger to the world? Didn't my dad tell me how many of the Marines in his own unit use to call him wetback and spick when he was in Vietnam? My dad also told me of a time his Sergeant commanded him to run through a small valley and my dad rejected the direct order. The Sergeant commanded another Marine next to my dad and got himself and the Marine next to my dad killed from poor judgment. Am I really wanting to join for myself or is it something else? To follow in my dad's footsteps? For myself? For pride or honor? For redemption? Do I want to join because I cannot think of anything else to do? Am I assimilated like most of my family? Is this my calling in life? Or do I have another calling?

All these questions Guillermo reflects on make his stomach turn. He feels as if he has been released from the chains of oppression to escape a cave of deceit and shadows that veiled his worldviews for so long. A prison cell has been his home – not in the literal sense of his juvenile rehabilitation center or the Junior Marines, but a metaphorical cell locked up within his own mind. The doubts, the anger, the sadness, the current and ancestral trauma of Guill's experiences growing up in a lower socioeconomic home limited his view of what he could do or become. Going to adult school and enrolling in college were all part of new seedlings that made him consider the world might be a lot larger than the confines of a cell he has been incarcerated within his own mind. For so long, his barrio, his experiences were *his* world and anything else was foreign and of no interest to him. This so-called *calling*, or dream, he put his focus into, he wants to join the best to be the best, he wants to be a part of the few and the proud, the Marines, just as they had advertised for young men like himself. But he began thinking that it may not be the best idea now. Just maybe, there was another way he could serve his community the way he wanted to serve his country. Perhaps the reason why he wanted to enlist was to simply help others rather than help himself and by helping others, he was doing himself a service.

He considers the feeling of being confined to his barrio and how trapped he feels living there. The drugs, the violence, the gangs, the religion, the subculture that he is a part of. Being confined within the walls of a juvenile detention center was anything but feeling free as well. But he found solace and freedom by working out his body and sharpening his mind through reading there. The irony Guill began to see is that a physical cell is not what keeps you confined, it's the cell of our minds that keeps us shut down and oppressed. The books he read while incarcerated were inspiring for him as many of the themes took him outside of his cell and facility into realities of the world.

Reading about the truth about the U.S. in Professor Martinez's class had a similar effect as he began to feel he was slowly breaking away from the captivity of colonialism. Martinez's class didn't make Guillermo hate America and that is not the professor's objective. The class actually made Guillermo feel like he was being released from centuries of bounded suppression – truth and knowledge that truly empowered why there are more people of color who are literally imprisoned as opposed to their white counterparts, the school-to-prison pipeline to where he and his barrio are no stranger to, and why the military is easily accessible in his hometown as well as his surrounding cities.

All Guillermo knew was that his first semester was going well, and he was going to attend a summer course to earn his 15 transferable units and enlist in the Marines. The peculiar thing is that his recruiter had not reached out. Guillermo wants to reach out to tell his recruiter how well he is doing – almost as if he craves the same acknowledgement Professor Martinez gave, but Guillermo suspends himself from doing that. A feeling to continue learning and embrace his life the pace it is going replaces the urge to call his recruiter. *After all, wouldn't the recruiter want to check on up their recruit? Maybe he's just busy. Eh, who gives a fuck.*

Part IV

CHAPTER FOURTEEN

The second half of the semester came to an end and on the last day of class, Professor Martinez wanted to have a quick word with Guillermo, "Guillermo, I wanted to run an idea by you. I don't ask this very often of my students, but I figured since you'll most likely be attending summer here, you can work on campus and make some dough on the side."

"Hey Profe, sure, but what exactly are you referring to?"

"Well, I have a knack for scouting out tutors for our tutoring center. You are a bright student as I am sure you have seen I've half mentioned that in the comments in your essays. Now that we are at the end of the semester, I wish to encourage you to check out our tutoring center and maybe consider a summer job. The supervisor knows me, and I am more than happy to write you a letter of recommendation if it interests you," Professor Martinez is happy to share the opportunity and hopes Guill takes interest in it.

"A tutor, huh? I don't know, sounds like a lot of work," the opportunity does not interest Guillermo all that much.

"It depends on what you see as work. When I come to teach, I truly never feel like I am working. Mainly because I enjoy my work. I get to meet interesting individuals like yourself and have conversations that not only keep me entertained but teach me different perspectives that are not my own. You seem to do a lot of work in your writing, and you explain things well. Those are two great characteristics of a tutor you already possess," Martinez explains – he also sees the characteristics of a teacher in Guill as well.

"Plus, it pays well. The tutoring center also works around your schedule since you'll be taking a class the last time we spoke about your plans. So, there's also convenience. But yeah, I just wanted to share that with you. No need to make a decision right now but think about it. If you have any questions, please feel free to ask."

"Thanks, Profe, muchas gracias por todo. I really mean it. This class really opened my eyes and taught me a lot and wish there was a part two," Guillermo feels cared for which he has not felt this feeling by another person other than his family besides Mrs. Rodriguez and his Dr. Thomas.

"Por nada!" Professor Martinez laughs with a great big smile.

"Its students like you that keep me coming back to this job. Also, I can still write you a letter of recommendation for you to become an officer for the Marine Corps when that time comes," the professor still wishes Guillermo to not enlist, but he knows he cannot force him. He knows he can try to persuade him to not enlist too, but as much as he would want to do that, he knows Guillermo needs to find his own path – the calling that draws him to what he wants to do with his life. One of Professor Martinez's philosophies whenever he does talk about the future with some of his students is to let students make their own choices, even if he disagrees with their choices. The positive side if Guillermo does enlist as an officer in the military is that he'll have a college degree, which will give him more opportunities. At least, this is what Martinez contemplates. Martinez also hopes that perhaps a subject in college may call to him just as community college called Martinez.

Guillermo bid the professor farewell but agreed to keep in touch. As Guillermo walked out of the classroom, a feeling of pride surged through his body. He feels that much prouder to call himself Chicano rather than a Mexican American. He takes pride in knowing he is among the few in his much larger family of thirteen tias y tios with countless primos to be enrolled in college and actually passing his classes. He doesn't feel a sense of superiority or "better" towards his family or homeboys he grew up with, as maybe some people attending college do feel; he feels lucky that he ended up in college not for the reasons to pursue higher education like so many 18-year-olds high school graduates do. He knows he dropped out of high school and his life could have gone in 100 different directions that could have made him another statistic or product of his environment, but he refused.

All of these feelings swarm his mind as he walks across the lonely, finals-week-driven campus back to his car. He looks at the American flag soaring in the lower campus nearing the parking lot as the wind makes it dance a rhythmic pattern. *So many people have died for that flag. My dad and grandfather fought and served for it too…* Walking on campus, knowing he passed his classes with 2 A's and 2 B's made him feel like he was on top of the world and when the idea of the American flag came to mind as it soars, flaps, and waves, he cannot help but feel a sense of guilt. Guillermo never felt this feeling before – feeling guilty for something he hasn't done yet but knows he will by enlisting into the military. The secrets the educational system this country chose to not teach or share – the very foundation of this country that was built on murder, lies, and deceit. But rather the American values taught to children represents bravery, loyalty, and freedom. *Utter bullshit*. The feelings of guilt began to dissipate and transformed into justified anger.

A new seedling was being nourished from this chapter of Guill's life. The nourishment that fed the seedling sprouting was the conversation he had with Professor Martinez for the midterm – the potential shared what he saw in Guillermo. For once, Guillermo feels like he has some value to contribute to society rather than be a body to be used for death or some war machine. It was also Mrs. Rodriguez's encouragement to not give up and, more importantly, to believe in himself. If it wasn't for her, Guillermo would not have entered the speech contest which led him to deliver the winning speech to his graduating class, an honor to embrace. And Dr. Thomas' care to set up Guillermo for success in the very beginning. Meeting a person of color who already served in the military and encouraged him to do his best was impactful and meaningful.

Most of all, the nourishment that did not let any of these interactions go to waste was Guillermo's commitment to moving forward. This was proof that he in fact can accomplish a goal if he puts his mind to it. And it also was his family whom many tias gossiped that Guillermo would amount to nothing, end up being incarcerated or join a gang, and then shortly after, say, they all needed to pray for him – he needed that part of his family to show him that not all family will be there to support and, in some cases, think the most ill. It was the homies in his barrio to where some loved and some hated him – he needed these opposite and intense energies to learn what was healthy to accept into his life such as a friend and the toxic relationships to discard that did not serve him at all. But most of all, it was the burning flame within himself – the fire – the very energy that he focused on to help motivate him to work hard and reach what he was trying to grab. Guillermo saw himself as the fictional Mexica Hero of his professor's Abuela's bedtime story, the great Cualli. His professor was the teacher he needed to make him consider not to take a path that he would or might regret later. Guillermo takes a deep breath out as he reaches his car and seriously considers that perhaps his path can be explored here within these college walls so that it can lead him to boundless opportunities.

Rather than enter his car, he stops and looks back to his college campus. He walks back to campus. Since it is the last day of the semester, passed all of his classes, he decides to visit the tutoring center. He has not made any final decisions of what he will do with the Marines, and if he is to enlist, he still needs his summer class. So, after all, what's the harm in checking out a place his favorite professor recommended to consider working over the summer? Guill enters the tutoring center and speaks to the supervisor.

CHAPTER FIFTEEN

Tierra decides to move forward with his decision to apply to become a tutor and earn some cash over the summer. Much to his surprise, he lands the job. The tutoring center supervisor, Rodrigo Nava, made the decision to hire Tierra as he admired his motivation to "work hard, be open to learning, and not be afraid to learn from mistakes," especially those from his past. Tierra is just the kind of person Nava looks for in hiring tutors, as they have to be disciplined, self-motivated, and willing to learn as they work with multiple students that have different needs and approaches. When Tierra gets the phone call from Nava that he got the job, Tierra was a little bit shocked. He thought he had a shot at getting the position, but his own traumas from his past and recent dealings put some doubts too.

The summer session for classes was going to start in about a week and Tierra prepares some documents to study a few days before going to his new job's orientation. Just as he delves into his papers, a phone call from his cell phone disturbs his preparation by an unrecognizable number. He ignores the number. *Spam calls.* It rings again. This time it is private to which does not change Tierra's mind in answering. A third time the phone rang, but he still ignored it.

Finally, a fourth time his cell phone rings, the calling from a stranger that is connected to something he once wanted more than anything else in the world, now calls because a quota is needed to fulfil. The calling stopped and Tierra continued his studying. About an hour later, the calling returned, and Tierra had enough.

"Hello?"

"Tierra?! What's up bro! I have been trying to reach you. You been trying to dodge me or what? We haven't heard from you. I'm calling since by now, you ought to have gotten those 15 transferable units by now, right?" Staff Sergeant Cocho now needs Tierra.

Tierra had passed all 4 of his classes which got him 12 transferable units. The summer introduction to literature class would give him 3 units, which would give him the 15 units he needed for the recruiters to help process him. This is a peculiar call that Guillermo was expecting in the back of his mind but forgot about as the semester kept him busy. *No, "Are you still interested, how has college been for you," or "how have you been?" Fucking prick asshole.* Guillermo wants to hang up as he remembers all the bull-shit Cocho put him through – all the hard work and effort Guillermo did, but to Cocho, "it's not enough, Tierra." Still, despite the whole process that led him here to college, Tierra has little strands of hope and ambition that have not severed completely to enlist.

He cannot help but give a white lie, "Yeah, bro! Got those 15 units. It was a challenge, but I got it done."

"That's what's up, Tierra! Hey, listen bro, we need you to come to the office to have you sign some documents. Check it out, we are getting you a boot camp date. Its official and we just need your John Hancock," the recruiter came to a dry spell where he now needs recruits to meet his quota, and Tierra would be an easy number to add, regard-less of the test scores that held him back to begin with.

Guillermo is conflicted since he has a job lined up and wants to take his summer course. Not to mention, he was told he needed 15 units, and the summer course would mean another month or so. Processing his emotions as to what he wants to do with his heart but also with what logically needs to get done in his mind, proves to be a dilemma.

"Wait, are you serious, Cocho? don't fuck around."

"As a heart attack. But the longer you wait, I don't know how long until another recruit will come in and take your spot," the recruiter sharply replies.

"Well, look, I have 12 units completed, the class I am going to take over the summer will get me 15, but I have the 12 units. Would that still prevent me from signing my contract?" Guillermo sounds anxiously worried.

"Mm, I thought you said you had it! I mean, the 15 would help you, *not me*," of course it will help the recruiter if a recruit shows a completion of 15 transferable college units, but he just needs Guillermo to fulfil a part for his quota.

"Having 15 units would get you meritoriously promoted in boot camp, but look, don't even trip on that, you may have time to still take that summer class. Just get here today and go over these docs with me," Cocho sounds anxious himself and it's bleedingly obvious to Guillermo.

This was it. The moment and time that Tierra stopped and turned his life around. The time he was able to make redemption from all the bad things he did. The realization that he proved to everyone who doubted him that he was a worthy human being. The point in his life where he would make everyone proud in his family and become a better person overall that society could respect. But at what cost?

Guillermo is learning something he never thought would be possible as a high school dropout – he actually enjoys college and it gives him a sense of fulfilment and purpose – continuing college might in fact lead to more opportunities just like Professor Martinez shared with him. Maybe he in fact could continue college and obtain his bachelor's degree and eventually apply to become an officer in the military. Why not? *I got my diploma when everyone including myself doubted I ever would. Look at where I'm at now. More money, probably more choices to choose from as an officer, it would just take a few more years.* Thinking about what he was doing in college excited him and gave him an itch of curiosity Guillermo felt he could not scratch anytime soon.

Moreover than what he remembered the advice about continuing school to become an officer in the military, Guillermo is rediscovering what it means to be Chicano. What he knew about identity in his neighborhood was superficial and he saw things for what they truly were. Chicano was so much more than the style of 501 jeans and oversized pro club shirts, lowriders, and kicking it with cholos, getting into mamadas, and doing transas – as a matter of fact, Guillermo was seeing how his own identity of what Chicano was misdirected and stereotyped. Being down for your hood and posting up was *not* Chicano at all. *Being* Chicano is about learning our history and ancestors. *Being* Chicano is about empowering our gente within our comunidad. *Being* Chicano is about being proud of our unique identity that embraces our Indigeneity and our Indigenous family all around us. Learning all these elements about Chicanismo and El Movimiento intrigues him, and one class will not suffice to continue this would-be path of embracing his identity, it takes a lifetime. If Guillermo goes with his original plan, he could always come back to college and the government would pay for his tuition, but what if he loses the interest he has now? That is very well a possibility. There were many what-ifs, but Guillermo is now in a position where he did not need the Marines nor want to enlist the way he wanted to a few years ago.

There was a pause as Guillermo had time to reflect on these matters within these months of the semester, "Cocho, I thought about it, and I think I am going to give college a try. I like where I am at right now. If I decide to enlist, I'll hit you up."

"Dude, what are you talking about? You have been wanting this for the longest time. You can always come back to college after your contract. Don't tell me your chicken shit now," the desperate recruiter replies.

Rather than Guillermo feel offended like he would before, even retaliate by insulting him back, he knew the recruiter wasn't worth giving away his peace, "Check it out bro, you blew up my phone today which me not answering meant I was busy. That shows no respect. You haggle me along for months, offer no help with tutoring me for the ASVAB whatsoever like other recruiters are supposed to, and you talk down to me like I'm already in the military. After I spent my time in juvi for my own shit, I go back to adult school and work my ass off and earn my diploma only for you to tell me I have to go back and redo more work because you can't read and understand what electives I took. You've given me shit since the start and now I am in college again proving that I work hard. And for what? For you to call me like *I owe you*. I don't owe you shit, and I am done with your bullshit. You are not only a shitty recruiter, but you also don't give a shit about the recruits, and it really does show. I thought the Marines were my calling in life, but you know what dude, I found another path. And trip out, I am glad I walked through your office doors since I chose to go back to get my diploma, because now, I am here in college on my own accord. Do not call me back," Guillermo hangs up and feels an immense surge of strength and power.

The Staff Sergeant attempted to call back twice,

most likely to tell Guill off, but he ignored both calls. He stood up for himself to a person who was a gatekeeper that did not care about Guillermo or his goals. He also did not care if Cocho and the gunny shredded and blacklisted his information in case Guillermo changed his mind to go back to the Marine Corps recruiting office or a different one. And he didn't care because he really feels in his heart that there is no more desire to give his life for a service that does not recognize and respect him, nor his own people. He read and learned plenty in Professor Martinez's class and the more he read up on how this country has treated marginalized and underrepresented people, it felt wrong to participate in the war machine's imperialized weaponry.

Guillermo took down the three posters of the Marine Corps he had in his room. He also threw away a shirt he got from the recruiting office, his keychain and other items that would remind him of joining. He felt free, almost as if the weight of joining the Marines were chains of being locked away. That pressure felt relieving to release. The night in Camp Pendleton when he saw the lava-colored gatling gun spray metal death from above returned to his mind. He feels there must be another way to *serve* and by service, Guillermo is interested how he can serve his own community – in a much different way than training to be a marksman with an M-16 rifle. And he had an idea of who to ask.

CHAPTER SIXTEEN

A day after his phone call with the recruiter, Guillermo looks up Professor Martinez's office hours over since he was teaching a summer class. The timing works perfectly as his professor's office hours would be open on a day when Guillermo does not have class or work. Guill decides to go visit Professor Martinez hoping he will be in his office. Martinez's door is slightly cracked and happens to be eating lunch.

Knock! Knock! Knock! "Hey Profe, hope I am not disturbing you."

Professor Martinez covers his mouth chewing quicker while nodding his head in disagreement, "N-Nonesense...g-get in here Guillermo!" He swallows the last chunk of chewed roast beef sandwich. "Que onda, Guillermo! How are you doing?"

"I am doing well, thanks Profe. How about you, how's the start of the summer?" Both are happy to see each other.

Professor Martinez clears his throat of the last of his lunch that may still be lingering, "Doing well! So, what honor do I owe this surprising visit from you?"

Guillermo really considered his options, and the idea was uncanny to himself at first, but it took a lot of courage and reflection to finally get the nerve to ask. Ever since the day of their midterm, Guillermo became curious to ask his professor something, "Well, Profe, I was wondering if it's okay with you, would you be able to share why you became a professor and what exactly do you have to do to teach here in the college level?"

Professor Martinez wiped his face with a napkin and smiled, "Did I ever mention in class where I grew up and how I ended up going to college?"

Both spoke at the end of Professor Martinez's office hours laughing, sharing more about each other's lives. Guillermo enjoyed the fact that his Profe and he had so much in common as it made Guill feel not only comfortable but also made Martinez more relatable. Guill began to feel like he could look up to Martinez and more importantly, felt safe around him. Almost as if he was a moral compass that could lead Guillermo to somewhere or something he could enjoy doing, perhaps teaching, although the idea of teaching for Guill is still quite intimidating. Martinez explained how he became a professor and the motivations that led him to where he is now and it was amazing to know how similar his background was to Guill; they both saw a bit of themselves in each other.

Guill could see himself teaching the more they spoke, and Martinez didn't need a quota to fulfil to help Guillermo become a professor – the Profe was beyond happy they were having this genuine exchange but still held no expectations. Committed to the conversation with his student lead to Martinez's sandwich being ignored and hunger forgotten. The Profe did not bring up the military and neither did Guill as it wasn't necessary, they both knew it was something of the past. Profe Martinez and Guillermo simply focused on the present – the start of the summer could not have begun any better.

Afterword

Thank you for reading *The Calling*. I truly hope you enjoyed it. Your support, dear reader, means more than you know and I am deeply humbled by it. Growing up the way that I did – succumbing to depression, experiencing suicidal ideation and suicidal attempts, dropping out of high school, going to a juvenile rehabilitation center, the countless mamadas I got myself into and stress I put my mom through, and so much more – I would have never suspected that I would be a writer. But through all the life lessons I have experienced, I am still here. I am a college professor. I am a poet. I am a writer. Since I was a chamaco, I always wanted to be a writer. My younger self saw something amazing with being able to open and flip through paper and ink that can transport the audience to a different world. Maybe the stories I read growing up kept me alive or helped me in some shape or form, who knows. What I do know is that my inner child is very happy. Keep that inner child alive and believe in your dreams. You may have to endure a few nightmares but do everything in your power to keep your dream(s) alive.

We need to share our stories and now more than ever, especially as Chicanx, Raza, Hijos del Maiz, LGBTQIA+, Black, Indigenous, People of Color. The more of our stories we share, the more we get to empower, inspire, and remind each other that we are all worthy and have a story to share, perhaps a dream to follow. This is what inspired me – reading a few writers that had similar stories to mine, reaching out to them and those writers not only replying, but also giving me motivational words. I hope that my story can hopefully do that to at least one person.

I wish to close by thanking you once again, dear reader, and by giving a special sneak peak of what's to come very soon…

Sneak Peak Poetry Preview of
Echoes de Aztlán
By Jacob Terán

You Are The First to Read This!
Enjoy!

Cosmic Nopal

Waiting for the sun's light to retreat to isolation,

Awaiting to embark from the docks of home,

Journey through the cosmos,

Climb the obsidian sky stairway, between the divide,

Above the concrete valley,

Under the ethereal cosmic and endless stars of Our Galaxy,

The lights from Aztlán can be seen.

Rested eyes on harmonious heavens,

Above cemented chaos streets,

Colossal figures play across the black field above,

Thoughts of past and future are blinks of an eye,

In the great cosmic scenery,

All is microscopic under the great cosmic canopy,

The vexations of life are inconsequential,

At this very second.

Existential search for purpose,

Unrequited answers from the tumult that is the world,

But soft resolve is revealed from the silences within,

To breathe and love is all,

Find any plateau and look at the cosmos and gaze,

Just as Our Ancestors did,

To breathe and love is all.

Colores y Sonidos de Aztlan

Colorful murals on the walls tell stories of Our proud Brown People,

Street vendors working in the urban jungle to make an honest living,

Esquite

Elotes

Tacos

Raspados

Chicharrones

With a mixture of pollution.

Families selling vibrant-colored flowers,

Tasty bronze churros,

All off freeway exits,

Taqueros on street corners with lines feeding empty stomachs to people of all ages,

Ice cream trucks with music that could be heard a block away that kids chase and shout at,

Paletas de sandia con chile

Lucas candy powder

Chips that leave your tongue and fingertips red-stained

Don't forget the bubblegum ice cream

We know this to be Our home

Because it is Our home.

If you ever visit,

Placasos on Our walls

In case you ever get lost.

Blood On a Block Corner

A quiet and peaceful summer night,

Car speakers suddenly blare as if a concert was bursting outside,

The music lingers for seconds that last a lifetime

Then, abrupt silence.

Followed by 8 loud vibrations that can be felt from my chest,

I jolt, run for the door outside

Half naked in a muscle-tee, boxers, and socks, I dash to the calle,

Tall man in his early 20s laying down on the corner street,

My homies live there

The music from the car is gone

No thinking, just movement.

My feet absorb the rocks from the floor, adrenaline blocking discomfort and pain,

The heart bashes the chest like a drum beating its way out

Heart rate is spiked, senses are at high alert

Reaching the corner block, my homie's oldest brother lays lifeless

Incapacitated from buffeted metal rain

Struggling to sit upward, groaning, tears of bemoaning death

Dark liquids on the ground encircle him, urine, blood, it cannot be discerned,

Left pinky finger almost decapitated hanging from skin and fragmented bone

The upper left thigh cries bloody droplets that shoot out like geysers.

Frozen from shock, I want to help but fear has incarcerated my body,

His mother comes out and shrieks in horror

The wounded man faints, his head thuds on the concrete

His mother wails to a sound I have never heard before and never longs to hear again

16 years of age, no more posting up out at night,

His mother's cry can still be heard in my head, if it is quiet enough.

Traumas Behind the Barrio Curtains

I see a man groaning in utter agony at the age of thirteen,
> Holding on to his right knee
> Full of burning pellets from a shotgun blast ripping and
melting flesh
> Sirens, helicopters, screams
> Fireworks, gunshots, I can tell you which one is which.

An older vecino getting his jaw broken from the boot of a jura,
> Handcuffed, stomach hugging the ground, the boot came
without warning
> Months later, stabbed in the neck from a broken crack-
pipe
> Fighting with his partner over who should get the last
hit.

I hear of an older neighbor throwing a brick at someone's face
during an after party,
> Skull fractured and wrecked permanently
> Disturbing snarls and snores came from the victim lay-
ing on his side.

I hear of my closest neighbor's brother who is shot in the right
thigh,
> We all stashed tall boys of cheap pisto in Our 501 jeans
from the local Superior
> Walked out like nothing, several times
> This time, not the luckiest
> Femur bone shattered from a hollow point bullet.

An acquaintance from a different barrio gets struck by an oncom-
ing truck,
> Short body flipping two times in the air on Olympic
Boulevard
> Getting up immediately, drunk, faints from the concus-
sion shortly after
> Drank and did every droga before he was 25

Dies at 44 not from the getting hit with a truck but from complications.

I hear 4 pops and a loud thud from next door while napping,
Gang in my barrio didn't like my neighbor's family due to street politics
My neighbor runs to his backyard, I can see him urinating on his hands
Removing any gunpowder just in case a case would open up.

I see a manchild point a gun at my neighbor after a heated argument,
Slightly squatting and looking both ways, the manchild rushes him
The sound of a 9mm getting cocked back
Fortunately, a pistol-whip sufficed instead of someone getting shot
Months later, the manchild almost dies from getting down with a man holding a knife.

You can see and hear a lot in the barrio,
And although every barrio is different
Much of the same happens that you don't always get to see
Behind the barrio curtains.

You Are Being Sent Away

The feeling of indomitability

Governed by youthful arrogance

Distributing large amounts of mid-grade herbs at sixteen

Delusions of being untouchable for so long.

Constant truancy alarmed the school counselors

Distributing weed put me on the gang's "initiate" list

Either jump me or tax me.

Run ins with law enforcement patrols emboldened me to craft my guile

Stealing my mom's car several times got me into plethora of trouble

Including a near-arrest to juvenile hall.

I'll never forget when they came for me

Sleeping on the couch sala, intoxicated, vulnerable

Two middle aged white men, black gloves on, awaited my surprise from awaking

The aroma of a burning Marlboro Light cigarette brought me to my senses

The same kind I used to bum off of from my mom

Both men looked prepared to restrain me

Or defend themselves.

You are being sent away, to get help

Ideas spun, tornados funneling confusion

Am I dreaming?

This experience is none I have heard of yet amongst my peers

Why me?

This can't be real.

A residential juvenile rehabilitation center for at-risk youth

3 months in, a planned riot occurred

Police came in with guns drawn, pointed at us

Utter chaos.

Misunderstood traumatized youth willing to revolt

Harming others but only harming ourselves more, traumas un-checked

No healing, wounds gushing open.

For those of us that have been incarcerated, we are not broken or hopeless

We learn to be strong and become cold as a defense mechanism.

I fought in public,

I cried alone,

I became strong, and there is hope for those of us that have come out.

I was hurt, ignored, and helpless

Self-sabotage, the remedy, hugged me with comfort

A consistent comfort that I knew the result of my choices

Pride, reputation, and ego.

It taught me these things and I have been healing ever since.

Brown Student, White Teacher

First day of semester in community college.

Scared, uncertain, feelings of an imposter

The teacher asks everyone, "What do you want your major to be?"

Some classmates say, "Business," others say, "Nursing."

My turn comes and I say, "Philosophy and English."

The white teacher scoffs and tells me, "How noble of you!"

Everyone in the class laughs, including myself.

I felt stupid and alone.

How can someone like me take on majors that would be this difficult?

I'll probably fail

But…

Something inside me wanted to challenge that scoff

I also wanted to see if a Barrio Kid like me could do it.

Six years later I return to my same community college to work.

I am on my way to becoming a professor.

I run into the same white teacher in the urine stalls

"Hey, professor, remember me – How's it going?"

"Yeah, I remember you! Finish school yet?"

"I did! I am working here now as a tutor."

"That's great! What did you study or graduate in?"

"Philosophy and English."

I'll never forget his countenance,

And the feeling of accomplishment.

The Calling

Semper Fidelis – a philosophy taught.

> Ideology that motivated people to fight for a purpose

> Convinced many people to serve a country, to fight for a country

> A country that stole, raped, pillaged, and murdered to get where it is at today

> A junior marine that wanted to follow in the footsteps of his father before him.

High school dropout with no remorse.

> Juvenile delinquent indulging in daily debauchery

> Drug dealing and violence normalized

> Incarcerated in a juvenile rehabilitation center

> Eternal issues with authority

> The corps was asylum from his self-destructive path.

Adult school diploma worked very hard for.

> Excitement and nervousness to enter recruiting office

> Adult school transcripts questionable under the eyes of uneducated eyes.

Social deviant that desired change.

> To grab the reins of life and steer in a better direction
>
> But semper fidelis was looking for "ideal" candidates
>
> Young man was not worthy with adult school diploma and ASVAB scores
>
> Recruiters denied him, a near-soul crushing defeat
>
> Attending college is quickest solution to joining uncle sam's corps.

Attends college reluctantly, to aid his situation with college units.

> Began to learn about things never before in school or his Barrio
>
> > Culture, Indigeneity, and interventionism
> >
> > Questioning his own identity and position in this very society.

He grew close to a small number of his professors.

> Encouraged him to finish college, maybe teach
>
> Started tutoring and fell in love with the work, working with students
>
> Hidden penchant for literacy.

Irony eventually knocks on the young man's door.

Recruiters hail to him

Bodies are needed for the corps

Just another quota and the young man knows this now

They called and called

But he never picked up the phone, until one day

Recruiters asked, "ready to ship off?"

Only to reply, "should have got me when I was semper fi, do or die"

Phone call disconnects

Part of romanticized dream dies too.

New calling in life allowed him to be who he wanted to be.

Brown Consciousness awakens his spirit

To learn who he was, who his Ancestors were, his history

His story

And how he saw himself in a very white country

He still served his Comunidad

He became a profe.

Running as a Form of Resistance

When you think about why banquetas were created

They were meant for La Gente to walk

But, not Our Gente in Our cities that we populate

Now that we, La Raza, have gained much agency over the years

There is a lot of work ahead for us to continue reclaiming Our Land.

We can run

We run from las juras, la migra, peligros del barrios, y nosotros, pero

We can run for a different meaning – con Proposito

We can run in Los Barrios for Comunidad y Orgullo

We can run in las calles for salud

We can run on banquetas para pasarla bien

So, we do run, and we run not from anyone

We run with Our Gente, Our Hermanos y Hermanas

With Pride as people drive by and look to see

People that look like them

That look like Us.

Our Barrios, Our Calles, Our Banquetas

We run and we will not stop

Stomping on the sidewalks that were not created for Us.

Nopal en la Frente

1

I grew up speaking English.

But, when visiting my grandparents,

Mom always told me to say,

"¿cómo está?" y "¡te quiero!"

2

Playing soccer in elementary school began to make me think.

Friends spoke both English and Spanish.

Through sports and camaraderie,

I was accepted,

Even though I could not speak Spanish.

3

My barrio allowed me to see the dark side of my culture,

But it also taught me the proud side of Our gente.

The language of the pachuco, ¡Orale!

Wetbacks we were named by the whites and whitewashed alike,

Pochos we were called if we didn't speak Spanish – "tiene el nopal en la frente,"

Chicanos we are.

4

Indoctrination from family, friends, and television,

Confusion ensues from all directions of the wind:

"You are Mexican American and have Portuguese blood."

Do we have family in Mexico? Where in Mexico are we from?

"No we don't, they all live here."

5

I stare at myself in the mirror and see all my features.

I am indio,

I am mestizo,

Of course, these names are not given by Indigenous People nor Our Ancestors,

I am Hispanic,

I am Latino,

I am slowly eliminating what I am *not* and they are not these things.

6

I am nōchtli that is vibrant and attached to the nohpalli.

The prickly pear that is small, bright, and stands out from the green nopal,

Protected from the spines of the nopal, I grow on the outside of the nopal's paddles,

Although I look different from the nopal,

I am very much a part of it in every shape and form.

This, I wholeheartedly embrace.

7

Mí español es mejor, pero,

It does not dictate my entire identity nor mí orgullo,

Seguro que es parte de mí.

I am the prickly tuna,

Apegado a Mis raíces.

As a Chicano, I am likewise attached,

proudly to my Indigenous Roots.

Why I Never Joined Mi Barrio

Part •

Young morro at 13,

The option to join the gang lingered

Yesca smoking rituals, alcohol theft, breaking into private property

All that was taboo, slowly became the norm

The older heads saw the youngsters as "futures"

False promises of power, respect, and pride

"Can't you see yourself posted with a .22?"

Building Our courage cheaply for a cowardly purpose.

But something else lingered in the fragile mind,

Quarreling with Raza for territory

Destroying the minds of the youth

Decimating the Comunidad within the Barrio, chale

Misery loves company and I saw it firsthand

Drug abuse – loving it more than one's own mother

Reacting like an animal

Lack of humanity.

My time came to get hopped in,

Venturing my hood to buy weed in the blackness of night

An older head served me, tweaked out of his mind

He always asked me when I was going to get in the hood

Consent is not a necessity for initiation

I managed to escape.

Learning and developing street rhetoric became my weapon,

An idol who was feared but not respected

He was never there to protect la Comunidad

Nor the morros

Definitely not the helpless

Absolutely not the barrio.

Two decades later, I ran into the same man,

I approached and hit him up

He remembered my eyes, shocked to see who I had become –

Someone not like him.

"I am a college professor now – un profe" –

He didn't believe me

But that didn't matter

I stared into his drug abused and violence-filled eyes

I know he saw the same young eyes he once preyed upon

Hope, pride, and brown shield of a leader that didn't succumb to being offered a cuete

Further disconnecting Our Raza did not work those years ago, nor that day.

He saw a proud Chicano.

My younger self would have been proud of me that day.

I know the barrio is.

Bold like the Mountains

Riding in the backseat of a car on a warm clear day

210 Freeway, no traffic for the driver – clear road and The Great Hills of the Tongva

All of its beauty to the north, all of the metallic pollution to the south of its view.

For some, they are known as the Gabrielino Mountains

Standing bold and strong, rugged without restriction nor boundary

Brown and Proud masses hovering as tall as the clouds

Playing with the Sun.

My view of the mountains fades as I head east

Still able to see my favorite mountains, but from afar

Hills as brown as the mountains I saw before comes to view

As I take passage – reflections of being surrounded by these beautiful brown giants.

How man-made highways were created

But could not destroy these beautiful brown bodies

I am part of these colossal behemoths

But do others that look like me feel or think the same? –

Feeling like we are all pieces to something as large as these parts of La Tierra.

If La Raza were to unite and awake from this oppressed and deathly slumber

Mountains would arise from the Anglo cities and highways themselves

Only to unite with the brown giants that were here first

And, still remain even after.

His Story Is Not History

For centuries there are those that teach my Culture,

Perhaps an affinity to Mesoamerican history,

Teaching a nationalist perspective for this country,

Not from or by Our People,

For far too long I have seen others try to teach me *my history*, and I've had it.

I do not want anyone to teach me lies from the past,

This fire to know who I was and where I come from – my fuel,

After all, my blood can be directly traced back to the Motherland de Mexico,

But there is more to *my story*.

Not white, nor ever felt what it meant to be "American,"

I was born in the lost Tierra de Aztlán, also known as, Tongva Land!

Genuine connection profoundly felt within what courses through my veins,

Evidence is simply gazing into the mirror.

This has led to why I dedicate my life to learning,

Consuming literature of my proud People,

Learning about the true history of colonization, and the practices of colonialism,

Reconnection to Indigeneity.

Rejoicing with those whose identities were detribalized, scattered,

Yet, finding solace in an identity that finds power in Ancestry,

Aiming to heal what atrocities colonialism has torn apart,

Teaching those who feel they cannot claim part of their Indigeneity became a manifested goal,

And learning to love myself and embrace my own Indigeneity is lifelong journey.

People of the Sun

Closest of Mis Tias once upon a time
Born and raised in Boyle Heights, not East LA – there is a
difference
Hung around the people from the old barrio, White Fence
Married twice, three kids, three primos of mine
Her appetite for books knew no ending
Devouring books – possessed intelligence like no other
Challenging me with questions that prompted more than
just a yes or no
Before her, I never thought about who I really was
Before her, I never heard of:
The People of the Sun.

Over the years, she became "enlightened"
Found her Christian "god"
No longer People of the Sun – now, children of the "*Son*"
Homophone, conveniently used
Disconnection from the Indigenous Spirit
Embracing ancestry is no longer precious
Salvation can replace any element from the past if it means
being "*saved*."

I began college, excited to learn about Chicanismo
Very first thing she shared
"Be careful in college, mijo, they will turn you into an
atheist."

"Brainwashing" dogmas more concerning, rather than
learning about Our People
A grand wonder if she ever remembers
Our talks about the People of the Sun.

Divide and Conquer

To take down a powerful being

You cannot take it head on

You must attack it in parts

Make it vulnerable before it can be weakened.

Our People have been subjugated, divided, and conquered

Through assimilated practices of religion, missions, and indoctrination

To serve a "higher purpose."

What better way to strip away an identity

Than to take language, culture, and way of life away, erasure

Rebuild people by forcing them to believe in something that benefits others.

Our History of injustice was committed not long ago when we consider the span of time

Now, more than ever, have we been divided

But are we conquered, totally?

The pride and consciousness within us all is born again

But we need to stop living in this illusion of a dream that we are accepted.

We must realize that injustices still continue to this day

Be Proud of who we are

Imperative to not stay silent

Jolt the Spirit within us all to remember

Many of us will remember, in time.

Pájaro Feliz

A tumultuous time of uncertainty and personal doubt

Dread of anxiety paralyzing like venomous bite from a snake

A walk to my car, interrupted by a chirping that sounded erratic

Behind me, above the building I lived in, a small bird flew

Creature of flight with bold coffee brown wings

A porcelain color belly that would only be vulnerable at a second's blink of an eye

Dancing in the air while its wings moved and swung to its own rhythm

Impressive somersaults, dashes, and barrel rows all throughout its pathway

All the while dancing magnificently

Singing as loudly as possible

Nature's performance, just for me

Nature's reminder to be in the moment

Just like this bird

Carefree

Happy

Not afraid

Free in movement

And most of all

Free

Free

Flying wherever it please.

Brown Consciousness

We are taught to hate Our Dark Skin
Assimilate to white culture.
Fooled to believe that Our Ancestros were brutish savages
But who came and invaded this land and stole it?
Killed, raped, and pillaged?
Depending on who is telling the story determines that.

For far too long, we have not been able to speak
Manipulated, beaten, killed, raped, massacred, but Our
People are still here, resilient.
This conquest was designed to destroy Our Cultura as well
But we still dance, sing, write, and share Our stories.
As much as the colonizer spirit lives within many
They will continue to see that design successfully through,
if we let it.

They saw and called the Night of Sorrows from their de-
feat; their made up truth
They attempted to write off their disgusting atrocities.
We know it was the Victorious Night de los Mexicas
And we also know Our Ancestors did not lose through mil-
itaristic might.
The diseases those european savages brought are what
helped them "win"
And just like today, symbolically, the colonized disease still
sickens Our People
However, more of us are becoming empowered.
Emboldened by the spirit of the Victorious Night de Los
Mexicas.
We are reclaiming Our identity, that which gives us power
Awakened by that very realized power within us.

And now that we have that power, I will not stay silent.

We can now speak and scream of the pain from Our Past
and Present
Share the silenced voices of Our Ancestros
Join me in awakening the spirit within us, Mi Gente
As there is much work to do.

Pain and injustice embedded in Our Memories
Past down from Our Mothers and Fathers
Generational trauma continues until we wake up
Until we heal.

We don't have to awake by force or abruptly
Feel the spirit of Our Ancestros within as we regain con-
sciousness from the colonized slumber
The natural remedy to aid Our Souls from toxins of the
white capitalist system that plagues us
Recognize that Our People have accomplished and left so
much for us
Remember that Our Ancestros' philosophy and way of life
was natural and empowering
For us as well.

Little by little as we awake
We can then finally start to heal.
The Sleeping Giant is slowly awakening –
Not the giant of assimilation that we thought for so long
The Giant Pride of Our Ancestros that has been here all
along.

Colibri Bronce

The hummingbird flies with strength and might

His colors are vibrant green with proud bronze skin

His battle spirit is honored by Huitzilipochtli,

His heart is touched by Tonatzin.

But the colors alone are not what attract others to the circle

It is the spirit within.

The warrior hummingbird dances as he fights

And fights as he dances

All the while embracing its windborne journey

Content with life

Not concerned with inconsequential worries

The dance and battle of life es la vida

El colibrí domina su capacidad para seguir volando

He surrounds himself with love, vibras positivas

The hummingbird is aware of the universe

And all the things it understands and makes sense of and all
the things it does not

The hummingbird lives in the vast heavens

And rests on Mother Earth

He lives not for the past nor for the future, but for today and today only.

The warrior hummingbird dances as he fights
And fights as he dances.

El colibrí guerrero danza mientras lucha
Y lucha mientras danza.

We Will Rise

The Spanish brought more than just horses, firearms, and wheat to Our Tierra.
> European savages brought brutality
> Enslavement, and genocide.

The missionaries thought that it was their "duty" to bring their religion to My Gente.
> An excuse to force, rape, and murder whoever opposed
> Hypocrites of what they call the "holy" and "sacred"
> This genocide that has affected Mis Ancestros, affects me too
> Generations of pain, torture, and trauma.

Generations of resilience and resistance are what I cry to remember.
> Our Indigenous Hermanos fought fiercely against the invaders
> Obsidian, flint, stone, wood, and copper
> Blood, flesh, and bone
> As well as pride
> Our Ancestros fought and won many battles
> Battles that are not taught in Our School's history books.

Our Ancestros from the north fought the same invasive enemies from the south.
> Our Native Brethren fought with dignity and bravery
> However, the European savages continued the devastation
> Aid of horses and firearms

In the name of their "Manifest Destiny
The invading colonizers attempted to exterminate
Our People in Our Land
But Our Spirits are strong
We found a way to fight back.
Despite the knowledge of terrain.
The invasive foreigners had the advantage
Their cowardly "victories" from a distance became
praised in history books
Rather than fighting with honor.

It was not until Our Native Brethren learned to use what the
invaders brought.
To ride as one with the horse
To utilize the firearm
To fight fire with fire
The invader feared the Indio, por que El Luchado
con el Corazón y el Alma
This same Fighting Spirit is within us all
That very drive to be bold in the face of adversity
To fight for the right Cause
We must All remember.

The same way that we have language and written word.
These are Our new Horses and Firearms
Our new Weapon
To fight against the injustices that still cling to Our
Lands
The pen is Our Arrow and paper is Our Bow
The knowledge of Our Ancestros and beautiful tra-
ditions becomes Our Spirit
We will not die, We will not forget, We will contin-
ue to live
We will rise.

Author Bio

Jacob "Jake" Terán is a proud Xicano living in the San Gabriel Valley, Los Angeles, a.k.a. Tongva Land. Terán is a 2nd generation Xicano who was born in Montebello, Los Angeles, east of Los Angeles. A high school dropout who was placed in a youth detention center for his own actions, Terán was on the pathway towards gangs and incarceration. The tiresome lifestyle to which he found himself in, Terán wanted something else out of life. He decided to enlist in the U.S. Marine Corps only to be rejected by his Armed Services Aptitude Battery test scores and Adult School Diploma that he worked tirelessly for. Community college was not an option and the last thing he fathomed was to enroll but decided to anyway. Higher education, critical thinking, literature, and most importantly, learning about his culture and identity as a Xicano became his newfound passion. Years of higher education led Terán to indulge his forgotten love of literacy and found his penchant for helping others with their academic writing as a college tutor. He continued his education while working several roles as a college tutor, ESL specialist, and supplemental instructor in multiple community colleges, including his public university of Long Beach. He graduated with honors, obtaining his B.A. in both Philosophy and English. The motivation from where and how Terán grew up created a fire to continue and eventually obtained his M.A. degree in Rhetoric and Composition. He is currently teaching composition to several departments in colleges that include indigenous and Xicanx literature to where he embraces working with students who are underrepresented. In addition, Terán is an advocate for social justice, self-care, and embracing the cultural identity of others. He currently lives in Tongva Land (San Gabriel Valley), where he is working on several projects about his experiences growing up in his barrio that deal with gang lifestyle, drugs, violence, and finding one's identity in a chaotic concrete jungle that he calls home.

Email: jteranwriter@gmail.com
Instagram: nopal_cafe
Author's Website: https://jacobteran.wordpress.com/

Photographer: Juan Daniel Gomez

Jacob Terán is an Azteca Dancer who keeps traditions alive.

Publisher's Note

Daxson publishing was created to help marginalized artists and their allies publish their work, so the world can hear their voice. The vision for this publishing house is to help people get their work out there, and not have them struggle finding their way through the publishing process. Everyone's voice deserves to be heard, and we are here to help. If you are interested in submitting a manuscript, email daxsonpublishing@gmail.com.

Support our cause! Buy our books at daxsonpublishing.com.